0 6 FEB 1995

From public housing to the social market

In this volume, Jim Kemeny develops a new approach to the comparative study of rental markets.

The framework used takes the concept of *the process of maturation* of non-profit rental housing as its starting point. It shows how two broad policy strategies have been developed to channel maturation in different ways.

These are the 'dualist' system of state control of non-profit renting, which residualises it and protects profit renting from competition. This strategy is used in English-speaking countries, and Great Britain, Australia and New Zealand are presented as case studies.

The other strategy is to develop a 'unitary rental market' by integrating non-profit renting with profit renting to create a single rental market. This strategy derives from the German concept of the social market, and Germany, The Netherlands, Sweden and Switzerland are presented as case studies.

Jim Kemeny shows how each system derives from differences in the representation of vested interests, is informed by different assumptions governing how markets operate, and gives rise to different sets of policy problems.

Offering a radical critique of the orthodox view, it is argued that the time is now right for English-speaking nations to abandon state control over cost renting and allow it to compete directly with profit renting, as in the 'unitary market' model. International in scope, this dynamic, innovative volume will be of great interest to researchers in housing, sociology and related fields.

Jim Kemeny is Reader in Social Policy at the University of Plymouth and Docent in Sociology at the University of Uppsala. He is author of several books, including *Housing and Social Theory* and *The Myth of Home Ownership*, also published by Routledge.

From public housing to the social market

Rental policy strategies in comparative perspective

Jim Kemeny

London and New York

First published 1995
by Routledge
11 New Fetter Lane, London EC4P 4EE

Simultaneously published in the USA and Canada
by Routledge
29 West 35th Street, New York, NY 10001

©1995 Jim Kemeny

Typeset in Times by
Florencetype Ltd, Kewstoke, Avon

Printed and bound in Great Britain by
Mackays of Chatham PLC, Chatham, Kent

British Library Cataloguing in Publication Data
A catalogue record for this book is available from
the British Library

Library of Congress Cataloging in Publication Data
A catalog record for this book has been requested

ISBN 0–415–08365–6

*This study is dedicated to all my colleagues
at the now abolished National Swedish Institute for
Building Research*

Contents

Tables

Preface

This book is a critical study of comparative renting and reconstructs the field along more theoretically explicit and conceptually developed lines. As such, the book can be seen as a natural follow-up to its more general predecessor, *Housing and Social Theory*. It is a study of one specialist area within housing studies that can be understood as exemplifying the wider task that faces housing researchers in developing more theoretically rigorous housing studies. The need for a book of this sort which attempts to escape from the dead hand of mindless empiricism in one area of housing is itself a lamentable comment on the state of the field of housing studies.

Unfortunately, comparative rental housing is no under-developed backwater of housing studies. I have not picked on an easy target. On the contrary, the area has engaged the attention of some of the finest and most respected housing researchers. The failure on the part of housing researchers to conceptualise this one specialist field in housing can, with a few outstanding exceptions, be repeated across the board in housing studies.

That failure is, of course, shared by us all. We are all, including myself, unwitting accessories to the fact. My earlier comparative work has all the shortcomings that I am critical of in the following pages. For this reason, too, the choice of comparative renting as my focus is not blindly random. It follows from a long-standing interest in trying to understand the international structuring of forms of tenure, and why there are such major differences in patterns of housing tenure between otherwise similar industrialised societies.

In *The Myth of Home Ownership* published over a decade ago I was aware of the distinctiveness of Sweden's rental market, and of its importance in understanding Sweden's internationally low rate of owner occupation. However, I did not realise that the Swedish rental market shared many characteristics in common with a number of other societies with low home ownership rates. Therefore, although I appreciated the wider implications I was not able to fully develop the theoretical significance of the Swedish rental system for understanding the distribution of households between the tenures. I remained stuck on a level of explanation that focused on the policy analysis of one unique country.

The manner in which I came to the realisation that Swedish housing was no international maverick, but only one of a number of countries that had adopted an alternative model of rental market organisation was largely deductive. It sprang from a deep frustration that the wider theoretical implications of what I had been terming 'tenure strategies' were not being understood by other housing researchers.

It seemed obvious to me that Sweden's radically different rental system was the key to understanding why the Swedish home ownership rate was so low. Yet the response to this was invariably 'very interesting, but so what'. Few seemed to appreciate the wider implications of the Swedish case.

The reason, I now believe, was that I was failing to develop a *theoretical* case that transcended a single case study. Nor was I able at the time to provide a conceptual framework through which to analyse this phenomenon. The reason for this was, of course, a combination of remaining stuck in a narrow case study policy analysis mode and my inability to show that other countries have pursued a similar tenure strategy.

The breakthrough came, interestingly enough, not inductively, as a result of stumbling on empirical data on other countries that enabled me to build up a theoretical framework. Rather, the process was the reverse of this. The breakthrough came when I turned my attention to developing a theoretical framework that would lead me to look for the relevant empirical data. And the challenge to do this became apparent to me during work on *Housing and Social Theory*.

I was, of course, aware that my strictures about atheoreticity in housing studies applied to myself as well as others. Indeed, in *Housing and Social Theory* I devoted a whole section to an autocritique of *The Myth of Home Ownership*. While writing *Housing and Social Theory*, and particularly during the very fruitful autocritique, I promised myself that once that book was out of the way I would address the frustrating issue of tenure strategies. Following the maxim 'physician heal thyself', I decided I had to return to my earlier interest and develop it theoretically to my own satisfaction.

My approach was deductive. I took the cases of Sweden and

Australia as extreme examples of polar opposite tenure strategies and attempted to extract the major principles that underlay them. Britain provided additional material as an example of a society whose rental system was going through a process of 'Australisation'. Indeed, initially I had intended the book would only use these three case studies, just as in *The Myth of Home Ownership*.

But what would this conceptual framework look like? I was much helped conceptually by the debates that were raging at the time over the relationship between the state and the market. This had flared up in the wake of neo-liberalist revanchism that reached its crescendo following the collapse of European communism.

Sweden had for long been characterised as the epitome of the interventionist state: the 'new totalitarians' in the words of one well-known Cold War tract. But the neo-liberalist hubris over state intervention in housing began to put Swedish rental housing policy on the defensive by the late 1980s. It was in this context that I began to read the political and social science debates over state and market with a view to applying its lessons to comparative rental housing analysis.

Once I began to compare the Swedish and anglo-saxon rental systems as *markets* a paradox quickly became evident. There was a striking incongruity in the way public renting was suppressed and prevented from competing with profit renting on the open market in English-speaking countries. This contrasted with the way in which cost renting was encouraged to compete with profit renting in Sweden.

This cast an entirely new light on the debates. Here were neo-liberalists deriding a rental housing policy for being interventionist when it would appear that the boot was on the other foot. Perhaps it was the rental systems of English-speaking countries that were in fact the representatives of the new totalitarians? Perhaps Sweden represented a brave attempt to construct a genuine free market in rental housing?

The more I considered the matter the more evident it became that neo-liberalist rental market policies were founded on the suppression of cost renting and sheltering profit renting from competition by hiving off cost renting into a state-run residualised command economy. I began to feel slightly embarrassed by the sight of British housing academics being funded by their government to export so-called housing 'know-how' in order to enlighten the natives of Eastern Europe: to teach them how to set up 'free' housing markets by destroying cost rental housing and replacing it with a residualised public rental sector.

It was therefore the political debates of the early 1990s that provided the seedbed from which the dualist/unitary conceptual framework was developed. And it was only after this conceptual framework had been sketched out that I turned my attention to finding other examples of the dualist and unitary systems.

This deductive approach was quite natural, since it is clearly not possible to find case studies unless one knows what the countries are cases of. That is, one must know what characteristics to look for in order to be able to identify countries that constitute cases of particular conceptual models. It was not enough to choose countries with low home ownership rates. It was necessary to know what to look for in the way the rental systems were constructed and functioned.

I quickly realised that countries with market strategies differ considerably from one another in the way their markets have been developed. This in turn led to refinements in the theory. Differences between countries with dualist rental systems have similarly facilitated refinements. But essentially the development of a conceptual framework was deductive, though extended and qualified with the help of inductive moments of analysis.

The deductive nature of the analysis reflects the fact that the key to conceptual development is to transcend existing dominant paradigms. Unless one succeeds in doing this, it will be difficult, if not impossible, to find the empirical evidence that is needed to support the theory. One will quite simply fail to recognise significant empirical evidence.

Researching this book has demonstrated to me in a particularly striking and dramatic manner just how the data we perceive are the products of our theories. This is probably the most important lesson to be learned from the research process in general and from writing a book of this sort.

Acknowledgements

I would like to thank Stuart Lowe and all those who took part in the seminar at the National Swedish Institute for Building Research on 23 February 1993. I would also like to thank Bo Bengtsson, Simon Duncan, Ingemar Elander, Ray Forrest, Hartmut Haeussermann, Peter Malpass, Alan Murie, Peter Somerville and David Thorns for their comments on earlier drafts or parts of this manuscript. The National Swedish Institute for Building Research provided generous support without which this study would have been impossible. I am also grateful for the use of the excellent facilities at the School for Advanced Urban Studies at Bristol University, where I was Visiting Fellow from 1991 to 1994.

On 1 January 1994 the National Swedish Institute for Building Research was abolished and the entire staff served with notices to quit. In its place two new university departments, with a combined size considerably smaller than the Institute, are in the process of being established. One will be for the physical sciences under the Royal Institute of Technology at Stockholm and the other for the social sciences under Uppsala University. Both are to be located in a third town, Gävle, where the Institute had been based, and will give employment to at least some of the Institute staff, if on much less advantageous research terms.

During the preceding decade the Institute had built up an international reputation as one of Europe's leading urban and housing research centres. I would like to take this opportunity to express my gratitude for the excellent research facilities that were provided by the Institute during the years of my tenure as Senior Research Fellow. The lively seminar series, the opportunities for research visits to other centres, the conferences held at the Institute, and above all the friendliness and strong personal support I received all contributed much to my further development.

Part I

From implicit anglo-saxon model to a theory of change

Introduction

With the emergence of two superpowers after the Second World War, Western Europe came under the cultural influence of the USA and its English-speaking allies. Cultural dominance in Europe is nothing new. The Roman Empire, pre- and post-revolutionary France, and, for periods, Austria, Germany and other countries have exerted powerful influences on the cultural, political, social and economic organisation of European society. But the post-war anglo-saxon[1] influence has been unprecedented both in its continental-wide impact, extending since the end of the 1980s from the Atlantic to the Urals, and in the speed and depth of its penetration.

This has been possible for a number of reasons. Improved communications and electronic media have given cultural dominance a more immediate and compelling impact. It has been further strengthened because US culture and language are shared by and originate from two European countries, one of which, the UK, is a major European power in its own right.

Cultural dominance has taken clearest manifestation in the spread of the English language and the increasing influence of US and British culture, including popular music and fashions, on European society. The influence is most tangible in societies which had, until 1945, been under German and Austrian cultural influence for several centuries. In such societies – and Sweden is a case in point – Berlin and Vienna have been replaced as sources of cultural inspiration by New York and London. In everyday life this is most evident in changing tastes regarding popular urban meeting places: the decline of the previously ubiquitous *Konditorei*, or coffee house, in such countries has been matched by the rise of the hamburger bar, and more recently by those owned by the big international chains, such as McDonald's.

More invidiously – yet much more fundamentally – there has been a largely unconscious assimilation of political and ideological perspectives. This has been most obvious in the impact of the new conservatism during the Reagan–Thatcher era. But that in turn is but the more dramatic and striking manifestation of deeper and more enduring political and ideological influences.

The spread of anglo-saxon conceptions of the profit-driven market is a classic example of this cultural imperialism. It contrasts sharply with the model of the market that has developed in Germany and a number of other countries. According to this 'social market' model, all markets – including those that are made profit-driven by hindering competition from non-profit organisations – must be policy-managed. In the social market model the economy is not seen as a sheltered preserve for unrestrained profit-making but should be exposed to direct competition from non-profit organisations. Both economic and social imperatives are recognised as of equal importance in the structuring of markets.

The starting point of this study is the way in which neo-liberalism has impacted on – indeed moulded – the dominant research agendas on comparative rental housing. I will first argue that current conceptions of European rental systems in comparative housing research are implicitly based on the profit-driven model of rental markets. In this model, social renting is kept as a government controlled residual form of housing for those least able to obtain housing provided by the profit motive. The alternative social market model is based on encouraging non-profit rental housing to compete directly with profit renting in order to dampen rents and provide a source of high standard housing on secure tenancy terms.

In applying an unexplicated neo-liberalist conceptual framework to all countries, much comparative rental housing research unwittingly contributes to the political debates in such a way as to foster and encourage the adoption by European countries of profit-driven rental markets that are sheltered from competition from non-profit rental provision. The corollary of this is that the social market system is not even recognised as existing, let alone highlighted, analysed and understood.

This is most dramatically illustrated by the impact of anglo-saxon housing 'solutions' on policy towards rental housing in post-communist Eastern Europe. The geo-political reality for these countries over many centuries has been that they have drawn inspiration from whichever Slav or German state happens to be politically and militarily dominant. The collapse of half a century of Soviet dominance in 1989 created a political and policy vacuum that was not filled by Prussia, Germany, Austria or some other German state, as had often been the case during historical periods when Russia was weak. Instead it was filled by the anglo-saxon dominance that was already established in much of Western Europe by that time.

Policies of privatisation, which result in the residualisation of the social rental stock have been adopted wholesale by East European countries, without any regard to the existence of possible alternatives, such as converting state-owned housing into smaller and competing autonomous non-profit housing organisations, whether owned by trusts or rental co-operatives. Indeed, anglo-saxon dominance has been so total that there is barely any awareness that an alternative to neo-liberalism even exists, let alone that any debate or discussion is possible over the strengths and weaknesses of the social market alternative.

The main part of this book comprises an attempt to develop a conceptualisation of rental markets and their historical development since 1945 that escapes from this anglo-saxon dominance. The dominant perspective in comparative rental housing research views rental systems as fundamentally more or less homogeneous with differences between countries treated as variations. This convergence model is inadequate since it attempts to force very different rental systems into the same analytical framework. As a result, the similarities are highlighted and the differences minimised and their significance is lost.

In place of this, I develop a view of rental systems in terms of the divergence of two principal types of rental systems, the anglo-saxon 'dualist' system and the germanic 'unitary market' system. These have corresponding policy strategies that I term 'command' and 'market' respectively. These policy strategies generate quite different sets of problems that must be overcome. The principal difference is that a 'rent-differential crisis' is produced in the dualist system while a very different 'rent harmonisation problematic' is produced in the unitary system. Each system is informed by a specific ideology and view of how markets operate and is the product of different kinds of power structures. I also suggest – though much more tentatively – that each system tends to be associated with a particular kind of welfare state.

The conceptual framework presented in the following pages must therefore be seen as part of a wider endeavour to develop more conceptually aware housing research. This can best be done by doing such research rather than simple exhortation. The study must therefore be seen as an attempt to escape from the barren empiricism with its implicit – and therefore unrecognised – theory that dominates comparative rental housing research and that pervades housing research in general.

1 Profit markets and social markets

INTRODUCTION

The profit and social market models represent contrasting approaches to social policy. The profit market model has its origins in the gendered conception of what used to be called 'economic man',[1] although later with the rise of sociology this became transformed into the wider gendered concept of 'rational man'. The social market model takes a more nuanced view of human nature. Economic activity cannot be seen as separate from other activities. Nor can any pure type of rationality be identified as the sole or even the major motivation for behaviour. Rather, different dimensions of personality and character are seen as constituting an indivisible whole. Economics, politics, culture, and the whole range of human experience meld in a complex and integrated symbiosis.

These two models of human behaviour underpin contrasting theories of the functioning of markets and are expressions of more fundamental world views or paradigms. Liberalism is, along with Marxism, an example of a one-dimensional economistic explanation of social phenomena in which other dimensions – social, political, cultural are subordinated. But in contrast to Marxism, liberalism sees markets as not just economically determined but more narrowly still, as driven purely by the profit motive.

The appalling consequences of the industrial revolution, when liberalism as a political ideology held sway, led to a massive reaction and to the attempt to develop alternative political economies. Two alternatives came to prominence. These were Keynesianism in which the state attempted to meliorate the effects of unrestrained profit-seeking by counter-cyclical measures and by constructing a safety net social security system and communism which attempted to replace the profit motive with state control.

Keynesianism therefore attempted to meliorate the social effects of unrestrained profit-seeking, while communism tried to replace it with state monopoly capitalism. So neither of these models escaped the economic determinism that underlay liberalism's market theory. Both models built implicitly upon a separation of economic from social, cultural and other dimensions of social structure.

Another, less well-known, model that was not economistic but multidimensional did emerge – the social market model. It was developed in Germany and, like liberalism, it viewed markets as governed by profit-seeking. However, profit-seeking was understood in its broadest sense of the pursuit of self-interest. This was understood to include private non-profit and self-sufficient forms of provision. It was also, crucially, seen as requiring state intervention to ensure that social as well as economic goals were attained.

The social market model underpinned the 'German miracle' but became little known and even widely misunderstood outside Germany. The failure of the communist model, the inadequacy of the Keynesian model and ignorance about the social market model have all contributed to a resurgence of interest in liberalism and the profit motive as governing markets. The last decade or so has therefore seen the re-emergence into respectability of the concept of the misnamed 'free' market

The concept of the social market not only provides a successful alternative model to the profit-driven market but, more importantly, has been particularly successfully used in the social construction of rental markets that differ fundamentally from the anglo-saxon model. This chapter considers the intellectual origins of the concept of the social market and the way in which German market theorists developed the social market model that came to underlie the 'German miracle'. It then outlines in broadest terms the principal differences between profit and social market conceptions of rental policy.

MARKETS AS SOCIAL INSTITUTIONS

The peculiarly strong hold that laissez-faire ideology had on social sciences in the nineteenth century derived from the ideological dominance of a combination of a patriarchal 'rational man' ideology and Social Darwinism at a time when the social sciences were still in their infancy. The concept of a 'free' market is one in which the profit motive – pursued under conditions of competition between profit-seekers – results in the balancing of demand and supply. It assumes that markets are detached from the impact of social and political institutions and from social relationships, whether in terms of class, ethnicity, gender or other dimensions of social structure. Most particularly it assumes that markets operate best when they are detached from the state and from legislative and political intervention.

The idea that economic institutions are, or should be, untainted by the social, political and legal structures of which they are a part must be understood in the context of the long-term process of social differentiation in which the economy in particular has come to be increasingly separated out from other aspects of social structure. The degree of autonomy of a market economy has come to some extent to be a measure of its development. Classical sociology has been much concerned to describe and explain this process of differentiation. Emile Durkheim, Max Weber and other sociologists saw the emergence of the market as a product of industrialisation that was driven by the process of social differentiation.

Max Weber, for example, in *Economy and Society* described how the factory system emerged out of the less differentiated household economy to constitute a separate institutional sphere. In the same way, bureaucracy was seen by Weber as a 'modern' institution, epitomising 'rational' behaviour. According to this, administration as a specific task is institutionalised and detached from such extraneous 'social' influences as friendship loyalties, charismatic leadership, and family and kinship obligations.

Although Weber did not fall into the trap of crude economism, it is but a short step for neo-liberals to argue that markets contain imperfections because they are still tainted by 'social' influences of one sort or another. They therefore retain elements of underdevelopment because they have not become sufficiently differentiated out from the wider social structure into specialised economic institutions. This is a common explanation of, for example, the existence of nepotism and corruption in Third World societies.

The solution to dealing with such 'imperfections' in markets is therefore to increase exertions to purge the market of all 'extraneous' influences. It is this that explains, to some extent at least, the vehemence with which neo-liberals insist that the state withdraw from market activities. Yet paradoxically, few, if any, neo-liberals would go so far as to argue that state involvement in markets can be totally eliminated: for example by repealing all legislation that impinges however remotely and indirectly on market behaviour.

Despite this, neo-liberalism's main impact on social policy has been to attempt to remove what are considered as extraneous social and political elements from the functioning of markets, principally through minimising state involvement in markets. The apparent rationale for this is that markets are more efficient the less state interference there is.

However, the argument to minimise state intervention is not what it first appears to be. The profit-driven market can only operate effectively if non-profit forms of economic activity are suppressed or discouraged from developing in the first place. It might therefore be more accurate to say that profit markets become more profitable the more the state intervenes to encourage profitability and the more the state discourages forms of organisation that are non-profit based and that might compete 'unfairly' to reduce profitability.

A serious consequence of creating a profit-driven market is that social problems become more acute. It is then often politically expedient and sometimes socially necessary to construct public sector safety nets to take care of those who become the casualties of the workings of the profit market. So alongside the profit market there develops a state non-profit sector that acts as a safety net for the profit sector. Instead of allowing non-profit forms to compete directly with profit forms, non-profit forms are hived off from the market and organised as a residualised state sector.

Neo-liberalism therefore displays two rather different and somewhat contradictory tendencies. On the one hand markets are desired to be as heavily profit-determined as possible. On the other hand the consequences of this are that the state is pressured to construct a set of safety-net provisions. These are kept as negligible as possible to discourage their use.

How extensive they become depends largely on the power structure of society and the relative balance between the desire to maximise the size of the safety net on the part of those representing the disadvantaged in society and the desire to minimise it on the part of those who wish to minimise collective responsibility for disadvantaged groups. However this conflict may be resolved, the result is that a curious dualism emerges between a largely unregulated profit-driven market that is sheltered from competition from non-profit forms on the one hand and a tightly controlled state sector that is based on non-profit forms of social organisation on the other.

Weber's description of the process of growing autonomy of economic and organisational spheres in society does not necessarily lead to the interpretation that this process needs to be driven to its extremes in order to enhance the development of society. Weber himself had a much more nuanced understanding of the relationship between different spheres of activity in modern society. This tradition has remained strong, especially in sociology and political science.

The concept of the 'free' (or more accurately 'profit-driven') market that has emerged from the disgrace it has suffered since the end of the Victorian era has come under increasing conceptual and theoretical attack by sociologists and political scientists since the late 1980s. Political scientists, such as Bowles and Gintis (1990), argue that markets can never be understood without reference to the exercise of power, both in its narrower political sense and in more general social terms. Fligstein (1990) argues that corporate strategy is not governed primarily by market considerations but rather by the strategic drift of public policy.

Sociologists tend to focus on the importance of informal relationships as a key enabling dimension of the functioning of markets. Silver (1990), for example, argues that friendship is not an extraneous social factor that intrudes on and distorts market processes but on the contrary underlies them, since it provides the basis for the spread of information about prices and quality without which markets would be much more ineffective. Granovetter (1973, 1983) argues that weak ties perform an essential informational function in enabling markets to operate at all. In short, the very functioning of a market is fundamentally dependent upon – and therefore cannot operate without – the existence of active networks of informal information based in the final analysis on relationships, friendships, gossip, rumour and mutual back scratching. This in turn is generated by informal relationships, between the insiders of different institutions in the give and take of news and information in informal settings such as bars and restaurants, and mediated by news-culling through networks of friends and relatives.

More recently, Granovetter (1985) launched a frontal assault on the assumption that economic institutions such as markets can be analysed or understood outwith the social structures of which they are a part. He coined the term 'embeddedness' to sensitise analysis to the fact that markets are inextricably part of society and that the structuring of the market is directly formed by the values, power relationships, and institutional arrangements of that society, both in terms of the social institutions out of which markets originally emerged and in terms of existing institutions with which market organisation co-exists and operates. Warner and Molotch (1993) use the concept of embeddedness to carry out a context analysis of financial press reporting on the 1987 stock market crash. They locate the primary insider explanation for the crash as being socially embedded

conceptions of markets, rather than on classical economic explanations based on prevailing doctrines of economic theory.

What this large and diverse body of literature argues is that in practice markets are essentially cultural phenomena, and that the norms
and standards of behaviour that govern them are to a large extent
a reflection of the particular pattern of social relationships that have
emerged in the social structures within which markets are located.
Markets cannot exist without the dense network of informal relationships that both constitute the information sources that enable
markets to function and that provide the moral codes – including,
for example, the need for bribery and nepotism – upon which transactions are based. Indeed it is both misleading and futile to attempt
to conceive of the social dimension of markets as something external
to the economic dynamic of markets. There is therefore a close
affinity between modern critics of neo-liberalism and the principles
that guide the policy structuring of the social market.

GERMAN ORDO-LIBERALISM AND THE SOCIAL MARKET

Social market theory attempts to construct markets in such a way as
to strike a balance between economic and social priorities and
thereby ameliorate the undesirable effects of the market from within.
Although, as already indicated, the idea of the social market derives
from post-war Germany, its roots go further back.

Social market theory developed in Germany in the 1930s as an
alternative to the extremes of classical liberalism and the command
economy (Willgerodt and Peacock, 1989). A number of economists
and jurists were concerned to avoid the extremes of the Nazi command
economy and so-called[2] laissez-faire that was followed with such
disastrous economic and social consequences during the Weimar
Republic. Critique was in particular directed at the command economy
of National Socialist Germany. The hope was that out of the inevitable
– as they saw it already in the 1930s – ruin of war that would follow the
temporary triumph of National Socialism they could develop a fresh
start based on new principles that would avoid both extremes.

The proponents of social market theory constituted an informal
college called *Ordo-kreis* (the Order Group), which published numerous works, including the *Ordo Yearbook*. These 'ordo-liberals' wished
to develop what they termed a 'third way'. That third way involved
constructing markets in such a manner as to ensure that important
social goals were built into the market – what came to be known as the

social market (*soziale Marktwirtschaft* see Barry, 1993). This was based on the principle that intervention in markets is necessary and desirable but that it must be *marktkonform* or 'market-conforming' (Müller-Armack, 1989, p. 84).

This concept is difficult to specify theoretically. But it is well illustrated with examples. If we take rent-setting in public renting as an example, then blanket rent pooling of the sort that is common in British council housing where all dwellings of the same size have the same rents, irrespective of locational and other factors, then this would be *marktinkonform*, leading to over-demand for some housing and under-demand for other housing which produces the 'hard-to-let' syndrome. Demand-sensitive rent pooling in which the rents of attractive housing were high while those of unattractive housing were low would, by contrast be *marktkonform*. Similarly, a blanket rent freeze would be *marktinkonform*, while a low-income housing allowance system would be *marktkonform*.

The social market perspective can be exemplified by the work of Röpke (1950). He argued (pp. 198–223) that effective competition must be based on the preponderance of a wide variety of small-scale operations, avoiding the gargantuan extremes of state monopolies and capitalist oligopolies. He stressed that the optimal size of units of production was that which was sufficient to fulfil the needs of a family or a small community. He cited, as examples of this, traditional independent peasant and artisan production. Röpke often cited Swiss society with its independent family smallholder and small business as examples of the sorts of markets that work best.

Markets should therefore ideally be composed of numerous small concerns operating in their own interests. Yet this diversity must be balanced by market-conforming intervention by the state. Citing Walras, Röpke argued that this requires a balance to be struck between 'the order of varied detail' and 'the order of the integrated whole', so that neither untrammelled competition nor state control dominated. This was to be attained by what he termed 'compatible state intervention' (p. 179) resulting in 'controlled competition' (p. 182). He termed this 'the third way', avoiding the extremes of capitalism and communism.

This 'third way' became a defining characteristic of the Swedish Social Democrats in their construction of Sweden's post-war welfare state. One of its architects, at least, Gunnar Myrdal, may well have been influenced by the ordo-liberals and was in turn considered relevant to some of their work (Meyer, 1989, pp. 246–7). Whether Myrdal was directly influenced by the German ordo-liberals is unclear. He did, however, have good German connections, as did many prominent Swedish academics and politicians at the time, and would almost certainly be informed of the major economic debates of the 1930s.

Social market theory therefore finds its practical application in a distinctive set of market policies that differ in principle from both the residualistic liberalist policies of the Roosevelt–Beveridge kind and those of the command economy. Ordo-liberals argued for 'managed markets' that would minimise the need for residualisation. This management would neither be subservient to the market nor try to determine and dominate it. Instead, it would 'be found in a "third" direction: neither in laissez-faire nor in intervention for preservation (obstructive intervention) but in intervention for adjustment (constructive intervention)' (Röpke, 1950, p. 187). Röpke described this with the following analogy:

> (Constructive intervention) neither wants to dam the natural course of development by the concrete walls of intervention for preservation – which will in the end give way in any case – nor does it wish to turn it into the wild falls of lassez-faire. Here, too, a third method will be adopted: the flow will be controlled and channelled, whilst its course will be shortened as much as possible. The pendulum which previously swung wildly from one extreme of laissez-faire to the other of obstructive intervention, will come to rest in a reasonable, central position of constructive adjustment intervention.
>
> (Röpke, 1950, pp. 187–8)

The social market model came into its own after the war under the economic leadership of Ludwig Erhard. Erhard was appointed head of economic affairs under the United Economic Territory (the combined US and British occupation zones of Germany). Not long after, he became Minister for Economic Affairs under Adenauer whom he subsequently succeeded as Chancellor of the Federal Republic of Germany.

Erhard, who was an academic economist by training, had followed the debates of the ordo-liberals closely during the 1930s and 1940s and maintained close contacts with its key representatives. In 1952 he brought the prominent ordo-liberal Alfred Müller-Armack into the staff of his ministry to lead a team of economic advisers which included several other prominent ordo-liberals. Müller-Armack was responsible for coining the term 'social market economy' (*soziale Marktwirtschaft*). He became under-secretary of state in 1958, a position he held until 1963. Erhard therefore became the political mediator for the implementation of ordo-liberalism during the critical early years of Germany's reconstruction. It was during this time that the foundations were laid for the post-war German economic and social order.

Ordo-liberals had been primarily drawn from among economists and jurists. Their main interest lay in constructing a market system based on rule of law that respected private ownership while encouraging benign forms of ownership. This included state ownership in areas of the economy where monopolies were deemed unavoidable – utilities such as electricity, gas and water being cases in point (Röpke, 1950, p. 190). But it also crucially included co-operative and non-profit forms of ownership.

Other disciplines such as sociology and political science were not well represented among the ordo-liberals. Nor were the ordo-liberals primarily social reformers or social administrators. As a result, ordo-liberalism had a very legalistic and academic economic approach to the problem of the construction of a social market. And because the concept of the social market constitutes a 'third way' between two extremes, it was quite difficult to charge the concept with ideologically powerful imagery such as 'freedom' or 'equality' as the two extremes of liberalism and communism were, however misleadingly, able to do. The social market therefore never received clear political formulation.

A further limiting factor on the spread of the concept of the social market is that it remained primarily a German phenomenon. It was an approach that emerged out of specific German experiences of the extremes of liberalism and nazism, and was well suited to the process of total reconstruction that both economic ruin and political discontinuity caused by the ending of the Second World War had made not only possible but necessary. In 1945 Germany was not only economically destroyed but, equally importantly, its political structures and party political organisations had to be rebuilt from scratch. The ordo-liberals filled an important vacuum in the recreation of a market economy along social market lines.

The inward-looking nature of German economic and social thought during this period was, of course, in part also the result of a realpolitik in which Germany's natural area of influence – Central and Eastern Europe – remained politically inaccessible. This was in part because of Soviet hegemony over Eastern Europe and the Iron Curtain. More fundamentally, it was the natural consequence of total military defeat. Yet the concept of the social market did penetrate outside Germany to a certain extent, particularly to neighbouring smaller countries such as The Netherlands, Denmark, Sweden and Austria. In particular, several prominent ordo-liberals, notably Lutz, Röpke and Tuchtfeldt, held chairs at Swiss universities.

The low policy profile of social market theory meant that it was widely misunderstood, and sometimes not even recognised as a theory in its own right, but merely as a variant of liberal interventionism. Willgerodt and Peacock (1989, p. 1) argue that safety-net Keynesians and Western socialists at first denied the success of the economic policies inspired by the ordo-liberals. Later the term 'the German miracle' was coined to indicate that the economic success of West Germany was inexplicable and took place in spite of misguided policies and a misguided theory (for an example of this kind of critique see Balogh, 1950. Balogh later became a close economic adviser to British prime minister Harold Wilson).

Social market theory differs from neo-liberalism in viewing markets as being embedded in wider social, political and cultural institutions. The task of government in such a system is not to encourage profit-driven markets and then construct emergency 'safety-net' arrangements to take care of its casualties. It is rather to actively take part in the construction and continual maintenance of markets.

In particular, it is to ensure that they operate in such a manner as to provide adequate welfare for the most disadvantaged and thereby to dispense with the need for a safety net that institutionalises and entrenches a disadvantaged underclass. Markets need to be structured in such a way that welfare is provided for without introducing unduly large market distortions.

An important part of this is encouraging non-profit forms to compete with profit-seeking forms of social organisation. To use an analogy, non-profit organisations are not separated off from the economy in the way that fat is separated from meat. Rather it is 'marbled' into the meat. The skill of managing this political economy lies in achieving this 'marbling' to maximise the benefits of both competition and social security.

The concept of the social market therefore involves policy making in continual monitoring and evaluation. To use a neologism, policy making is 'proactive'. Markets need to be subject to a process of structuring and re-structuring to ensure that they function as efficiently as possible. At the same time they need to be constructed in such a manner as to minimise the problems that this creates for society as a result of the marginalisation of sections of the community created by unrestrained market forces. The aim is to achieve a reasonable balance between economic efficiency and social welfare needs. Social markets therefore need continual managing in a manner that reconciles requirements that may sometimes conflict with one another.

The success of the social market model for German economic recovery after the Second World War provided a model for a number of other countries to follow. Indeed, the countries which have adopted the social market model have been among the most successful of industrial European societies in terms of economic performance in the post-war period. This is certainly true for those countries that have social rental markets. Indeed, it is in rental markets that the social market economy has taken its clearest and most enduring expression. Most other areas of the economy have tended to lose their distinctive social market character. This may well be due to the need to develop oligopoly to compete internationally, a factor which does not figure in terms of rental housing provision.

PROFIT AND SOCIAL MARKET RENTAL STRATEGIES

The different strategies towards the rental market that are described next reflect the profit and social market perspectives. In the chapters that follow these strategies will be examined in detail from a variety of angles. In this section the principal outlines of the strategies are described.

Profit market policy strategy strives to construct a rental market that is based entirely on profit-making principles. However, there are strong political pressures for governments to maintain some sort of regulation over profit renting, and so continued rent control and other regulatory measures have remained a common and enduring feature of profit rental markets. Even so, there is generally little or no room for cost-based operations on any significant scale in such a market.

The result is wild swings between rampant profit-making during times of housing famine and massive disinvestment during housing gluts. Both result in marginalisation on a substantial scale. To handle this situation the state then creates a cost rental sector which it runs. Cost renting is thereby hived off from the private rental market by the state and is used as a safety net in the form of a tightly controlled public rental sector.

Ironically, then, the concern to minimise state involvement in the rental market involves the state in taking over responsibility for an entire sub-sector of the rental market. The very act of encouraging and creating a profit-driven market marginalises – and at the same time creates the need for – a social rental housing sector. Governments are invariably then pressured to provide cost rental housing to fill the gap between demand and supply.

This may vary in size from a few per cent to a major form of housing provision, depending on how fanatically the profit market doctrine is pursued and the extent to which the social costs of such a market are accepted. But it appears that some form of cost rental housing is a universal feature of housing in countries which have a profit rental market. It would seem that governments in every industrial society have found it necessary to provide such housing.

But creating a state-run cost rental sector is not sufficient to solve the problems created by a profit rental market. It is then necessary to continually be on guard in case the public cost rental sector threatens to grow and increase its share of households in indirect competition with the profit-based part of the housing system. In order to prevent this from happening, state control over cost renting becomes harder and closer and takes on suppressive functions. This centralised state control gradually restructures the public rental sector into a command economy.

The inability of the profit rental market to provide adequate housing for ordinary households combined with the reluctance of a government pursuing a profit rental market policy to allow state-run cost renting to fulfil this role impacts directly on household preferences. A residualised public rental sector which is both unattractive and stigmatised and, because of strict means-tested access, is not a realistic option for most households to enter, leaves the choice between profit renting, with its high rents and insecurity of tenure and owner occupation. A rising demand for owner occupied housing is thereby created. The profit market strategy therefore has the effect of heavily structuring the demand for housing towards owner occupation.

Policy therefore creates a rental system that – perhaps at first unintentionally – steers household choice towards owner occupation. This in turn creates a consumer 'preference' for owner occupation which then leads government into a policy of actively encouraging owner occupation as a response to demand. There is no attempt to develop neutral government policy which allows household choice on the market to determine the relative balance between owning and renting. Instead, the housing market is structured in such a manner as to maximise the number of households in owner occupation.

The result is a self-fulfilling prophecy in which the more that one-way biases are built into tenure choice the more households will begin to express a 'preference' for the policy-favoured housing. This preference can then be seized upon to explain why the policy measures had been introduced in the first place.

But which comes first, the policy that creates preferences or the preferences that, through the ballot box, lead to the policies being endorsed? It is this chicken–egg phenomenon that is ignored by those who attempt to explain the existence of policies in terms of attitudes and preferences. It is the results of the endorsement process, not the preference-formation process that is measured by researchers such as Saunders (1990) who argue that policies favouring owner occupation are introduced because they are popular.

The result is quite the opposite of the 'small-state' ideal of neo-liberalism. The route towards the creation of a marginalised public rental sector is, however, tortuous. Its steps may be spelled out as follows:

1 Public policy encourages an unhindered profit rental market to develop.
2 This results in the marginalisation of sections of society.
3 This puts pressure on governments to assist the households so affected.
4 The state creates a cost rental sector to cope with this.
5 It is kept segregated to shelter profit renting from its competition.
6 This is not sufficient to keep demand for rental housing down.
7 As the public cost rental sector grows and matures, relative rents fall.
8 State control is then tightened to stop cost renting from expanding.
9 This diverts demand from renting to owner occupation.
10 Government increasingly encourages owner occupation.

In the social market model, encouraging cost rental housing to compete with profit rental housing is an important part of creating a diverse and competitive rental market. Additionally, a large cost rental sector provides a significant ameliorating influence on the rental market as a whole. It does so both because by ensuring a steady supply of new housing it helps even out the wild swings from glut to famine and because its cost-based operations dampen market rent levels.

The lower rents also make possible a shallower subsidy system that is less selective and discriminatory. A major problem with rent allowances in a profit-driven market is that they may aggravate already high rents by increasing demand without doing anything to increase supply. At the same time, cost rental housing offers a high degree of security of tenure and high housing standards. Profit rental landlords are obliged by market forces to take account of this in operating in a mixed market. Indeed, a central feature of the social market is that private landlords receive significant subsidies. Often, though not necessarily always, subsidies to profit-orientated landlords are tied to obligations to meet certain minimum standards of construction, security of tenure, and sometimes rent levels. The net result is a rental market in which the worst excesses of the pure profit market are avoided.

A distinguishing characteristic of social market rental policies is that sophisticated forms of rent regulation are developed that apply to both profit and cost rental housing organisations. Their most important characteristic is that they are *marktkonform* rather than the crude application of blanket rent controls as is used from time to time in, for example, English-speaking countries. Market conformity is achieved in a number of different ways, as we shall see in more detail in Part II. For now we may merely note that in Sweden the aim has been to achieve a rent structure that reflects use-values within a cost covering framework. In Germany and Switzerland a system of comparative rents operates which reflects existing – cost rental influenced – rent levels, and so is interactive.

Another difference is that in contrast to profit market policies that favour owner occupation, the social market rental strategy does not presuppose any sort of over-riding public goal as to which housing tenures should receive political favour and which should be suppressed. Cost renting is not reserved for safety net functions. Nor does the policy aim to achieve some preconceived percentage of owner occupied households. Instead it strives to encourage cost renting to compete directly with profit renting and also as part of this strategy to create an even playing field between the tenures in which renting is not penalised nor owner occupation favoured. Under these circumstances the balance between the tenures is determined by household demand rather than by governmental fiat.

ON DOMINANT VIEWS AND RESEARCH PARADIGMS

These contrasting world views are also almost entirely unexplicated. This is partly the result of the widespread unreflexive adoption of the dominant neo-liberalist paradigm as the intellectual prism through which rental markets are analysed in the English-language housing literature. The more a policy strategy can be taken for granted as unquestioned and unquestionable the more powerfully entrenched it can remain. Spelling out the grounds of the dominant policy strategy lays it open to query and provides the perspective and concepts necessary to formulate counter policy strategies and alternatives. So the less explicit the policy strategy is made the smaller is the area to dispute and to become a subject for public debate and a focus for opposition.

A deeply entrenched policy strategy can gain the legitimation – even if often unwitting – of housing researchers simply by housing researchers failing to unmask and explicate the grounds of that policy strategy. If the political strategy is sufficiently deeply entrenched it will be unthinkingly adopted even by those not particularly sympathetic to the policy strategy simply because its ideological slant is unrecognised as such and no counter-strategy can be conceived of.

Herein lies the explanation for why certain policy strategies in certain countries have such political clout. They constitute part of a wider ideological dominance in which the truth is defined in such a way that the policy strategy remains unquestioned, self-evident and 'natural', as, for example, Saunders (1990) succeeds in implying is the case with Britain's dual rental and pro-home ownership system.

This is most blatantly obvious in the case of a command economy in public renting being instituted in the name of protecting a free market. This paradox is not seen as inconsistent or indefensible because the mode of discourse in which the policy strategy is couched does not admit to the existence of a 'command economy'. The very idea is anathema. Nor is there any alternative mode of discourse to unmask this paradox.

This disadvantage is reinforced by the tightening centralised political control that results from instituting a command economy in public renting. Then the disadvantaged and centrally controlled rental system is used in the nature of a self-fulfilling prophecy to justify why public renting is inefficient and needs to be further reduced, or if possible eliminated. And because the policy strategy is not even recognised as such, there is not even the language to critically evaluate the claims made for the dominant policy strategy, let alone to make possible the formulation of alternative policy strategies.

2 The Romeo error in comparative renting

INTRODUCTION

Before embarking on the main part of the analysis, there are a number of prior issues that need to be clarified, by way of ground-clearing. These derive from the conceptual and perceptual confusions that have arisen in comparative rental housing research as a result of the combination of the ethnocentricity and theoretical under-development that characterises housing research in general.

My argument in this chapter is that ethnocentrism resulting from the absence of explicit theorising has led rental housing researchers to interpret the symptoms displayed in social market rental systems as indicating the same fundamental structural problems as exist in profit market rental systems. The absence of conceptual guidelines for analysis leads to the phenomenon of 'pattern recognition' that has been described as part of much scientific analysis and that contributes to the stubborn persistence of traditional paradigms even after they have been challenged (Margolis, 1993).

In terms of the analysis of rental systems this phenomenon of 'pattern recognition' is reflected in the manner in which, for example, cost rental housing in the social market is interpreted as equivalent to public rental housing, and disproportionate numbers of lower income earners in cost rental housing is taken as evidence of the same residualisation as exists in public renting. Inductive ethnocentric interpretations are thereby imposed on the data, which are made to serve as a sort of Rorschach blob (i.e. selecting the researchers' own unexplicated preconceptions). Defining the data in this way leads to the search for more data to confirm the pattern and to neglecting data that does not 'fit' with the preconceptions guiding analysis.

The conclusion that is drawn is that the two systems are to all intents and purposes identical to one another. The mistaken diagnosis of death that constitutes a key part of the plot in Shakespeare's *Romeo and Juliet* is therefore also made in comparative rental research by a misreading of symptoms which leads to an erroneous diagnosis.

A more general critique of housing research as it is currently constituted is presented in Kemeny (1992a). That broader discussion will not be dealt with here. Suffice it to say that the problems in the field of comparative rental housing research that are discussed in this chapter are but a specific expression of the deeper malaise of contempt for theory in housing studies in general.

The limitations in our understanding of how rental markets operate is a dramatic illustration of the profoundly empirical and atheoretical nature of so much housing research. Abstracted empiricism is not, as Wright Mills pointed out some thirty-five years ago, purged of theory as some of its practitioners might believe. Rather, empirical work is deeply permeated by a world view that takes the form of an implicit explanatory framework that is often not even recognised as such.

The very implicitness of the theory gives it great durability and strength. Work that is explicitly theoretical and makes clear the conceptual basis used exposes the researcher responsible to evaluation and critique. Work that embeds its theoretical and epistemological grounds in the data and presents the data as though they were objective findings that 'speak for themselves' is much harder to penetrate.

Anyone wishing to evaluate the theoretical basis of such research must first decipher the implicit theory. The potential critic must then make out a case to convince others that the research is, indeed, based on the theory the critic claims to have unearthed. Only then is it possible to develop explanations that derive from different theoretical perspectives. The first task facing anyone wishing to progress knowledge in the face of implicit theory is therefore to make explicit the implicit theory that is embedded in existing empirical research.

The first part of this chapter is devoted to excavating the implicit theoretical assumptions of comparative rental housing research. I therefore begin with a discussion of the fairly sparse literature on comparative rental housing. I then re-evaluate the traditional discourse of research on rental housing in the section on defining terms. I argue that the very language we use is profoundly influenced by the implicit theory that dominates housing research, and propose a different terminology that is more adapted to the explicit and alternative theory presented here.

THE ANGLO-SAXON BIAS IN COMPARATIVE RENTAL RESEARCH

Empiricism and implicit theory

Comparative European housing research is heavily influenced by the specific British experience, despite growing conceptual awareness among housing researchers. This influence is largely implicit and unarticulated. It is partly understandable with the early lead that Britain gave in developing more comprehensive housing policies, and the large size from an early date of its public rental sector.

However, there are more fundamental epistemological reasons for this influence. These derive from the under-theorised and unreflexive nature of much housing research that encourage an extensive and deep-rooted – yet unwitting – ethnocentricity in comparative housing research. The dominance of a thorough-going empiricism does not, as Wright Mills has pointed out, exorcise theory. This is because 'the everyday empiricism of common sense is filled with assumptions and stereotypes of one or another particular society; for common sense determines what is seen and how it is to be explained' (Wright Mills, 1970, p. 138). Empiricism more invidiously leads to the entrenchment of unexplicated paradigms which at best slant empirical work in particular theoretical directions and at worst encourage what I have termed elsewhere 'theorisation by innuendo' (Kemeny, 1992a, p. 57).

This is particularly true of the literature on comparative renting, which, however, is fairly limited in size. There are only a handful of contributions to this particular topic: Harloe (1985), Emms (1990) and most recently Power (1993) being the main ones. Saunders (1990), while not about comparative rental housing nevertheless draws far-reaching conclusions about the future of renting in general and public renting in particular and so must be included in this literature.

The literature, which will be briefly reviewed below is a particularly striking representative of abstracted empiricism. No theories are presented with hypotheses that may be tested. Concepts are few and far between. No conceptual frameworks are developed. Few, if any, questions are raised. Controversies and conflicting interpretations of the data are all but unknown. Instead, rental housing systems are seen as unproblematically unfolding. The data speak for themselves. This means that the analysis is largely descriptive. Objective facts are gathered and presented, commonly in the form of voluminous tabulations.

The unanimity among scholars concerning the nature of a topic that is so controversial and emotionally charged as rental housing and the absence of any conceptual problems or debates must be viewed with great suspicion. Is the social organisation of rental housing markets so unproblematic? Are the rental systems of all industrialised countries essentially the same? Is research on rental housing needed merely to catalogue in greater and greater empirical detail the unproblematically describable rental systems of more and more countries?

This is, I would suggest, most unlikely. Rather, the apparently unproblematic nature of rental systems conceals important conceptual problems. The descriptive analyses must therefore be understood as glosses that conceal deeper structural issues in the organisation of rental systems.

One example of this is the descriptions of historical processes of change, which are glossed in such a manner as to highlight their shared characteristics. Where differences cannot be glossed over they are described, without any attempt to explain them in other than idiosyncratic terms, as 'variations' thrown up by culturally specific forms of social organisation and as being historically unique combinations of events. If anything, the existence of such variations serves to underline the shared characteristics while demonstrating an awareness of a more fundamental yet ultimately analytically elusive complexity.

Yet behind all this atheoretical descriptive analysis must clearly lie a set of implicit theoretical assumptions that guide analysis. I wish to suggest that researchers are using an implicit profit market model of rental systems, the net effect of which is to make the anglo-saxon system of renting applicable to all rental systems.

The reasons for this are twofold. In the first place, the literature fails to recognise the conceptual significance of the distinction between cost rental housing that competes with profit renting and cost rental housing in the form of segregated public renting. Secondly, it assumes that all rental housing is undergoing similar broad processes of decline and residualisation. In particular, it is assumed that cost renting suffers from comparable problems, and that it is in a state of more or less permanent decline. The taken for granted assumptions of the British experience are thereby unwittingly used to explain processes in housing markets in other countries.

The common argument behind these views builds upon anglo-saxon – and in particular recent English (as distinct from British) – experience in which private renting has undergone a long-term decline in size while public renting has been significantly cut back in more recent years. It is argued that this decline is not specific to English-speaking countries but is being brought about by exogenous forces that cannot be reversed or even halted by policy measures. The explanation for the assumed inevitability of the decline of renting is therefore to be found in general social or economic factors that are not clearly specified. This structuralist argument must be understood, in part at least, as a reaction against what Ball (1983) has termed 'the politics of tenure' with its narrow focus upon the tenure effects of public policy.

Recent more conceptual work on housing has therefore tended to emphasise dynamics that the rental systems of all countries are subjected to and that are seen as deeper and more structurally rooted in the economy or in the human psyche than policy making. Indeed, to a certain extent, it dismisses policy as largely irrelevant to understanding the nature of housing provision in its broadest sense. Thus, for some, such as Castells (1977), Harloe (1985), and Ball *et al.* (1988), the exogenous forces that mould the rental market are to be found in the profit motive and the dynamic of capitalism. For others, and most notably Saunders (1990), they are to be found in a psychological or even instinctual preference for ownership and a natural resistance to renting.

These viewpoints, in spite of major – not to say fundamental – differences in their approach, share two assumptions concerning rental markets. They are that renting is in a state of irreversible decline, and that this decline cannot be understood either in terms of the internal organisation of the rental system or in the policies of governments. Instead the decline must be explained by wider social, psychological or economic factors. In both the 'logic of capitalism' and the 'human nature' perspectives, the decline of renting is presented and explained as the result of inexorable processes in the wider society that are beyond the means of housing policy to fundamentally alter.

The two assumptions that underlie the literature – that there are two rental tenures and that renting is in a state of structurally determined decline – will be considered in turn.

Renting: one tenure or two?

Ball's critique of tenure-fixation notwithstanding, the assumption in the comparative rental literature is almost universally made that public and private renting effectively constitute different forms of tenure. This amounts to treating them as different from each other as owner occupation is from renting. This 'three tenure' model of owner occupation and two rental tenures is very pervasive in anglophonic housing research. I wish to argue that this assumption results in the unwitting perpetuation and reinforcement of 'the politics of tenure' approach.

We need to bear in mind here that 'tenure' refers to the form in which domestic residential property is held (the word tenure coming into the English language, via feudalism, from the French verb *tenir* – 'to hold'). That is, tenure defines the rights and obligations of the household (literally 'the house holder') rather than the manner in which the housing is provided.

Yet if the provision perspective (Ball and Harloe, 1992) has conceptual value then it lies precisely in distinguishing between forms of tenure and forms of provision. Within one form of tenure – such as renting – it is possible to distinguish different forms of provision – such as private and public. It follows from this that while different forms of provision of the same tenure can lead to differences in the conditions in which households hold their dwellings, this is by no means inevitable. Differences in forms of provision can, and often do, result in variations in the conditions in which households hold their dwellings between housing in the same tenure. However, for these differences to become so great that two separate forms of tenure emerge out of one requires much more than this, including, I would argue, legislative and judicial support.

Indeed, it is partly because private landlords have resisted granting security of tenure to households that the public rental variant of the rental tenure was originally introduced. Differences within the same tenure both in terms of provision and conditions of tenure can in some countries become so extensive that the cumulative result is to create what amounts to different forms of tenure. However, this cannot be understood outwith the policy-making process.

This is particularly the case in Britain, where private and public ownership of rental housing has become closely connected with very different forms of provision, in terms of finance, subsidy system, rent-setting and allocation. This has resulted in the terms under which rental housing available from different kinds of providers is held (conditions of tenure) developing major entrenched differences, notably in terms of the degree and type of security of tenure, rights of disposition, tenancy transfer, and rights to buy. Nominally private and public provision may be variants of the one tenure defined as 'renting', but the differences between them have become so fundamental as to effectively create two tenures out of one.

There are therefore convincing grounds for arguing that in English-speaking countries public and private renting do indeed constitute different forms of tenure. However, it is also important to recognise that this dualism is not an inherent characteristic of renting but a specific cultural product of the way in which the housing system is organised in such countries. In particular, it is the result of the entrenchment and institutionalisation of wide variations between the form of provision of public as against private rental housing.

These variations have in the long run become so extensive and far-reaching that they have altered the conditions under which housing in the two forms of rental provision are held. Over time, then, the institutionalisation of differences in forms of provision have lead to diverging conditions of tenure, to the point at which rental housing originating from different forms of provision possesses such differences in its conditions of tenure that it can convincingly be seen as constituting different forms of tenure.

This process is, crucially, the product of a politico-legal construct, since it is the result of cumulative legislation and policy over many decades that entrench and reinforce such differences rather than attempting to minimise them. Systematic divergence between forms of provision within a type of tenure is therefore the product of cumulative legislative and judicial decisions over extended periods of time.

Yet although the divergence between public and private provision has been a characteristic of British rental housing, no generalisation can be made that different forms of provision of rental housing in other countries have necessarily diverged to produce different forms of tenure. Merely because there is a strong case for this being so in English-speaking countries does not mean that the assumptions can be extrapolated to all other countries.

Yet this is precisely what comparative analysis often does, more by default than intent. The anglo-saxon model of segregating and sharply differentiating private and public rental housing constitutes the basis for conceptualising private and public renting as different forms of tenure in other countries for comparative purposes.

Thus, Harloe (1985) and Emms (1990) are both studies of renting in a number of countries. But Harloe (1985) is a comparative study of private renting while Emms (1990) is a comparative study of social renting. Both authors thereby take the anglo-saxon model of the rental market as their starting point and design and delimit their respective comparative research agendas in terms of the culturally specific conditions that exist in English-speaking countries.

Of these two, Harloe makes clear that he is aware of the conceptual issues at stake and is critical of the politics of tenure approach. However, he justifies, somewhat unsatisfactorily, focusing on private renting as 'both practically necessary and of some empirical validity' (Harloe, 1985, p. xxv). At the same time he does not question the assumption that different forms of renting (public and private) can be assumed to be different forms of tenure for international comparative purposes.

Despite this, both Harloe and Emms point to countries in which the distinction between private and social renting is unclear. However, they do not consider the differences significant enough to modify the neo-liberalist paradigm accordingly.

Thus, for example, Harloe (1985, p. 61) points out that the classification into private renting, social renting and owner occupation as used in the book 'is rather misleading, unless carefully qualified' and that 'The German housing market fits least comfortably into the broad classification adopted here' (Harloe, 1985, p. 63). Harloe returns to this point time and time again in different contexts.

Emms (1990), too, alludes to the more integrated nature of private and social renting in Germany. He states that 'private landlords, both individuals and firms, in Germany can also provide subsidised social rented housing' (Emms, 1990, p. 119). He further argues that in The Netherlands private landlord companies who charge controlled rents (tied to historic costs) 'provide an extension to the social rented sector on a similar basis to many private landlords in Germany' (Emms, 1990, p. 192).

Yet, despite this clear awareness of the inappropriateness of the two-tenure renting model, no attempt is made by either author to develop an explanatory framework that systematically takes account of the more integrated nature of profit-oriented renting and cost renting in these countries. Rather, the differences are treated as 'variations' on the basic neo-liberalist theme: epiphenomena that demand qualification of the neo-liberalist model but do not invalidate it.

Much the same can be said for Power's (1993) study of housing – primarily cost renting – in five European countries. However, perhaps because Power goes into each case in considerably greater depth, a much more nuanced picture is presented. Indeed, Power stresses how the different forms of rental provision – primarily public renting, cost renting and private renting – vary between the case study countries.[1]

She notes that the two anglophone countries of Britain and Ireland contrast sharply with the other three countries of France, Denmark and Germany, having larger public rental sectors and minimal cost and profit rental sectors (Power, 1993, p. 10). In spite of this, Power does not attempt to explain or even to theorise these differences. They are simply presented and noted. And because the book is about 'state-sponsored' or 'social' housing which can – and often does – include all forms of rental provision and it concludes that there will be a continuing future for this form of housing, the significance of the differences between the countries is effectively overshadowed.

The inevitable decline of renting?

The division of renting into two tenures – public and private, with certain Continental 'variations' is coupled to a view of 'public' renting as being in a state of decline and marginalisation. Again, here British council housing seems to be the implicit model that is being applied. The model is reinforced by the fact that public renting in the other English-speaking countries is much smaller than in Britain and much more residualised. The sense that social renting everywhere is moving in the same direction appears to heavily influence the conclusions that are drawn about other countries as well.

Thus, Harloe (1985, p. 314) argues that there are 'tendencies – more developed in some countries than in others – for social rented housing to become marginal or welfare housing, limited in supply and beset with problems'. More recently, Harloe (1993) has emphasised the residualisation of social rental housing even more strongly. Emms (1990, p. 7), likewise, points to social renting undergoing an 'accelerating spiral of social decline in the western countries'. Private renting is also in 'seemingly inevitable decline' (Harloe, 1985, p. 311), and the net beneficiary of the decline in both kinds of renting is the owner occupied sector. Power (1993) suggests that social rental housing will increasingly concentrate on the provision of housing for groups with special needs.

A distinction needs to be made here between the empirical observation that renting in many countries is undergoing contraction and the implicit theory behind this apparently innocent observation that extends the fact of the structural decline of renting in English-speaking countries to other countries that may have different rental systems. It may well be the case that renting is undergoing contraction in many countries, but it does not follow that this is for the same systemic reasons as, for example, in Britain.

More specifically, in a system where the balance between renting and owner occupation is not being politically steered, changes in the proportions of tenures may vary over time. We will see later in the discussion that this may happen for a number of reasons. The most important of these during the first half-century following the Second World War is that cost renting is a relatively new form of housing and so bears higher costs. However, as we shall also see, there are cyclical factors at work that are so long-term in nature that shorter-term changes are easily misinterpreted as more deep-rooted lineal trends.

My point is that the observation that renting 'is in decline' may well be accurate in a narrow sense and when removed from more deep-seated trends and tendencies. The problem with such an observation is that in the absence of a conceptual framework to understand what processes induce this it is easy to fall into the trap of applying an anglo-saxon explanation to this process. This happens as a result of generalising from the experience of the kind of rental system that English-speaking countries have. That experience provides the implicit conceptual framework for interpreting phenomena that appear on the surface to be similar but may be quite different.

Saunders (1990), does not base his argument on comparative empirical analysis, since he uses solely English data. Instead he argues out of certain epistemological assumptions that similar processes are at work in all countries. He argues that the process of marginalisation and residualisation that is taking place in British council housing as a result of large-scale sales into owner occupation is the result of the search for ontological security. He thereby decontextualises the explanation of the spread of owner occupation in England from the specific national social structural factors of his empirical study and develops instead a generalised theorisation of the phenomenon. Saunders therefore implies – though he never actually claims explicitly – that his explanation transcends the British experience and applies to all tenures in all countries.

So strongly entrenched is the anglo-saxon model in housing research that it is adopted by authors describing Sweden, where renting is organised along quite different lines from those in English-speaking countries and where differences between the provision of public and private renting are not sufficient to class them as different forms of tenure (Elander, 1991; Lundqvist *et al.*, 1990. For a critique see Kemeny, 1992b, 1993). They adopt this model despite the fact that they themselves are natives of the country, the housing system of which they describe.

ETHNOCENTRISM AND IMPLICIT THEORY

Herein lies a paradox. Researchers who live in and research on the rental housing of a country with a quite different rental system to that in anglo-saxon countries nevertheless adopt conceptual categories that have been developed in English-speaking countries.

The reasons for this have much to do with the cultural dominance of the English language since the Second World War. As in most other fields, so much international comparative housing research is conducted through the medium of the English language, in international journals, other publications, and in major conferences. This makes anglophonic research much more widely available to the research community than research in, say, French or German. This is particularly important in smaller countries where housing research is well developed, such as The Netherlands and Sweden. In these countries English has replaced German during the post-war period as the second language.

This gives greater accessibility and prominence to the work of native English language researchers and their ideas, with the inherent danger this entails of unwitting cultural bias, particularly in a field of research where theory is scorned and discounted and where the emphasis is on empirical description. Indeed, even French and German research on comparative rental housing is often carried out and presented through the medium of English. And as far as research on renting in Europe is concerned, the specific British experience is particularly prominent. Much the same goes for other parts of the world with emerging industrialised and urbanised economies, such as Hong Kong and Singapore, where housing policy has been heavily influenced by the housing policies of colonial administrators.

This means that researchers taking the British experience as their point of reference will interpret the often very different housing systems of other countries in the light of the British experience. Three major ethnocentric interpretations can be distinguished as follows. (1) Since English-speaking countries possess a 'public' rental sector, other forms of organisation of cost renting are seen as merely variations of the public rental model. The significance of the difference between state controlled public renting and autonomous cost renting for the overall organisation of renting is lost. (2) Since public renting in English-speaking countries is effectively a separate form of tenure from private renting, this dualism is transposed onto other countries where it is less appropriate or perhaps not appropriate at all. The significance of the relative homogeneity of renting for how the rental market operates is lost. (3) Since public renting in English-speaking countries caters only for the most needy households and is effectively residualised and marginalised – or as in the case of Britain is becoming increasingly so – any tendency for cost renting in other systems to cater for a disproportionate number of low-income earners is interpreted as demonstrative of the same trend there. The fact that large groups of middle-income households live in cost rental housing fades into the background and its significance is lost.

The Romeo error lies in the mistaken belief that the loved one is dead, and drawing pessimistic conclusions from erroneous observations. Comparative rental researchers may be accused of the same mistake in drawing pessimistic conclusions about the future health of renting in countries with different rental systems from their own. They have hitherto tended to draw hasty conclusions about the future health of renting based upon their interpretation of the symptoms that the rental system of their own country has displayed. But this assumes that the displayed indications are, indeed, symptoms of the same underlying condition as those with which the researcher is used to diagnosing back home.

The main symptoms in question are the observed tendencies in many countries for the size of the rental sector to decline, and for the socio-economic composition of renting to become more heavily orientated towards low-income earners and households on social security incomes as a result of higher-income earners moving into owner occupation and other tenures. In English-speaking countries such symptoms are unproblematically the result of the residualisation of public renting.

I will argue in a later chapter that while these tendencies may exist in social market systems they are symptoms of a different underlying condition. This has to do with the manner in which these markets operate. In particular it has to do with the existence of cycles of production that are generated by the changing balance between profit and cost rental housing. This issue will be returned to towards the end of the book when the dynamics of social rental markets which underly this phenomenon have been discussed. For now I wish simply to indicate that the interpretation of symptoms in social market systems by drawing on the experience of the rental systems of English-speaking countries is fraught with dangers of ethnocentrism and misinterpretation.

ON DEFINING TERMS

Before developing an alternative perspective to that derived from the anglo-saxon paradigm, it is helpful to define some terms. As we have noted, in English usage, renting has traditionally been divided into private and public categories. Differences in rental provision have been defined in terms of whether the dwelling is owned privately or 'publicly': that is, by central government, local government, or some other public, or quasi-public agency. In English, then, private renting has come to be associated with profit-orientated landlordism while public renting has come to be identified with housing provided by some kind of public agency.

However, in recent years another term has come to enjoy wide currency in English, namely that of 'social renting' or sometimes just 'social housing', the meaning of which remains elusive. This confusion reflects the lack of analytical clarity in this area. The terms 'social renting' and 'social housing' are not labels developed to describe a conceptualised perspective as, for example, is the case in the social market philosophy developed by the German ordo-liberals. They are merely a way of describing (rental) housing that is provided for vaguely 'social' purposes and, to some extent, this label-switching is a symptom of the deeply ideological nature, in the English language at least, of much of the discussion over the role of renting. But it also reflects the fact that a diversity of types of renting has emerged over the post-war period which makes the distinction between private and public ownership less useful than it used to be.

This is the case, for example, in Britain, where the emergence of housing associations with their semi-autonomous status has made it inappropriate to either equate them with council housing or identify them as a form of public renting, and where a different umbrella term is seen as needed to cover all forms of rental housing that is not profit-orientated. In other countries cost rental co-operatives have a similar marginal position between private and public forms of rental provision, being non-profit yet not in some form of public ownership.

'Social renting' therefore seems to encapsulate forms of the organisation of renting in which the private–public ownership distinction loses its usefulness. This may be because private renting has an important social dimension or because a range of housing providers have emerged that are neither publicly owned nor profit-orientated. The term 'social renting' therefore seems to be loosely used to refer to forms of renting that transcend different kinds of ownership of rental housing while either retaining broadly non-profit aims or being intended for housing special groups.[2]

More invidiously, there has emerged an elision between the terms 'social renting' and the wider term of 'social housing'. Emms (1990) entitles his book on social renting *Social Housing*, and there is even a British journal with the same title which, confusingly, is devoted to the study of social renting rather than social housing.

This elision is unfortunate since much owner occupation could be termed 'social'. Substantial subsidies are paid to owner occupiers, for example, in tax privileges and in selling public rental housing at large discounts to purchasing sitting tenants. In addition, a range of policy measures are often taken to provide a public safety net for owner occupiers (for example against mortgage default).

Referring to social renting as social housing therefore creates an artificial distinction between 'social' and 'market' forms of housing that obfuscates more than it clarifies. It invidiously reinforces the belief that owner occupation is somehow a 'market' form of housing and is not subsidised. By the same token, it can also convey a suggestion that social housing is somehow a form of welfare. None of these terms are commonly defined or specified.

The term 'social housing' is not used in this discussion, and I have tried to limit the use of the almost equally vague term 'social renting'. I will continue to refer to public and private renting where this is appropriate and an accurate description of the form of rental provision in question. But in addition, I will use the term *cost renting* to refer to all rental housing, irrespective of ownership, the rents of which cover only actual incurred costs of a stock of dwellings. This may be achieved by a number of different means, such as rent regulatory legislation or political decree or because of the charters or policies of particular housing organisations.

By the same token I will use the term *profit renting*, irrespective of ownership, the rents of which are largely or entirely unregulated and where the aims of the owners of such rental housing – whether these be private individuals and companies or the central or local state – is to maximise profits in the form of returns on the current capital value of residential property.

It needs to be emphasised here that the distinction between cost and profit renting has some marginal problems of definition. It is possible, for example, to conceive of some forms of profit renting where profit levels are restricted – or even eliminated – by competition from cost rental housing. As we shall see later this is a key characteristic of certain kinds of rental systems. There are also hybrid forms of organisation that are profit-orientated but only up to a modest level. These are sometimes called 'limited dividend companies'.

In addition, it is not always completely clear what is meant by 'cost-covering' rents. 'Reasonable' management costs, for example, is a flexible category. It can be argued that without local competition for households between different cost rental housing organisations there is little incentive for managers to economise on the costs of their own contributions. These will still show up as legitimate costs in the accounts but could well be grossly inflated. The boundary between cost and profit renting is therefore not entirely unproblematic, nor is it always fully apparent which housing can or cannot be called cost rental.

The main point of the usage is, however, that the distinction quite deliberately shifts the focus of attention away from who owns the rental housing. In so doing, it constitutes a valuable corrective to over-simplified assumptions that invariably public rental is synonymous with cost rental while private rental is synonymous with profit rental. State-owned or state-controlled housing can be – and increasingly is – run on a profit generating basis, just as privately owned rental housing can be run on a non-profit basis.

This usage emphasises instead the extent to which rental housing organisations – irrespective of ownership – allow tenants to retain high levels of imputed rent. These accrue as a result of low rents rather than being extracted in the form of higher rents which are expropriated and transferred elsewhere. 'Elsewhere' may be into the pockets of a private landlord or those of shareholders. However, it might just as equally be to a local or central government exchequer in the form of a negative subsidy or implicit tax on tenants. As we will see, the economic dynamic of the maturation process of cost rental housing has meant that such exploitation of public rental housing is becoming increasingly common.

These terminological problems vividly illustrate the way culture is infused into language. It is very difficult to discuss renting in the English language without using concepts that are specific to anglo-saxon housing policy and its political, social and cultural ramifications. They have, understandably, evolved and developed to reflect conditions on rental markets in English-speaking countries, particularly as they existed in the early post-war period when it was less usual for public rental housing to be used as a milch cow by central or local government.

It might be added here that the problem is not only that of communicating research in the English language: it also applies in other languages. The invasion of the English language into other languages and the need to communicate in a non-English language in a way that makes sense to anglophonic findings, debates, and arguments, makes for very substantial importation of concepts from anglophonic research. As a result, a sort of linguistic hegemony is established which sets the parameters of the debates and provides an implicit conceptual framework that defines the research agenda.

3 Policy constructivism and the concept of maturation

INTRODUCTION

In this chapter I outline a conceptual framework to escape from ethnocentric anglo-saxon explanations of the organisation of rental systems and their trajectories of change. In particular, I am concerned to escape from the implicit view in comparative rental research that rental stocks in all countries manifest the same tendencies towards convergence and that social renting in all countries is moving towards a situation where the same problems of residualisation and marginalisation are becoming increasingly acute.

I develop a frame of explanation for the differences that exist between countries that adopt the neo-liberalist philosophy and those that adopt the social market philosophy. The dynamic that I focus on can be broadly described as the interaction between the economic development of rental housing stocks on the one hand and long-term strategic policy making designed to influence and channel that process on the other.

This is a complex and ever-changing relationship. Changes in the economic structure of housing stocks can act as the catalyst for the development of strategic policy responses to handle them. They can equally themselves be the product of changes in the direction of strategic policy. The different historical trajectories of the interaction between strategic policy making and changing economic structure of the rental stocks is largely responsible for generating the substantial differences between countries in the manner in which their housing systems are organised.

FROM STRUCTURAL DETERMINISM TO POLICY CONSTRUCTIVISM

As argued in the previous chapter, the anglo-saxon paradigm that dominates the English-language literature depicts rental systems as follows: (1) as characterised by a process of largely inevitable and long-term decline at the expense of owner occupation (and to a lesser extent other forms of tenure such as co-operatives) that it is largely beyond the power of government policy to prevent; (2) in which public and private renting constitute distinct and quite separate forms of tenure; (3) and in which public renting tends to undergo a process of increasing marginalisation and residualisation. All of these are, of course, not coincidentally, conditions which pertain to the rental systems of English-speaking countries.

I wish to challenge this paradigm and develop in its place the beginnings of a theory of the dynamics of rental systems. Within this, the anglo-saxon system in which two parallel rental tenures have developed is just one of two contrasting policy strategies for the organisation of rental markets.

I will argue that at the most general level, two dynamics interact with one another to produce characteristic rental systems. The first is processes of changing economic structuring which stocks of rental housing undergo over extended periods of time. The second is long-term housing policy strategies which interact with power relationships to impact on the social organisation of renting in a systematic manner over long periods of time.

The interaction between the economic development of rental housing stocks and their long-term policy structuring determines the trajectory of development that rental housing systems follow. The way a rental system develops will therefore be the result of the interplay between processes of economic change in rental housing stocks and the development of policy strategies to channel that change.

The channelling of the development of rental housing has profound implications for the manner in which the whole housing system is organised. In particular, some ways of channelling the development of rental housing will stimulate the development of other tenures, and notably owner occupation, while others will inhibit this. The key factor here is whether a rental system is developed which is attractive to households. A rental sector will be attractive if rents are cost-based and there is high security of tenure, and if supply is allowed to expand to meet demand. Such a rental market will be highly competitive with owner occupation and will retain a large proportion of households, including better-off households.

I term this perspective on the long-term process of politico-economic structuring *policy constructivism*. I contrast it to the dominant structural determinist school of thought in the comparative rental housing literature. According to the latter, neither the economic development of the rental stock nor its judicial/legislative organisation play a significant part in the formation of rental markets.

Structural determinism is an over-reaction against a one-sided focus on narrow political analysis. It throws out the baby of policy strategy together with the bathwater of the narrowly defined 'politics of tenure'. Policy constructivism attempts to redress the lost balance by re-emphasising the importance of long-term policy in interaction with economic processes within rental housing stocks for the structuring of tenures.

Policy constructivism therefore views rental systems as undergoing identifiable processes of economic growth. These are characterised by cycles and phases of development, that can be channelled and directed in different directions by various policy strategies. The application of a particular policy strategy structures the further development of the rental system, channelling future growth in certain directions or stifling growth to enforce decline. Over decades or generations consistent policy strategies can profoundly affect the organisation of rental housing, and thereby also that of the housing system as a whole.

The processes of economic change that stocks of housing undergo is reasonably predictable. The policy structuring of this process of economic change constitutes the element of variability that can transform and direct this process of change in a number of different ways. The policy structuring is itself, of course, strongly influenced by wider power relationships in society, a point that will be developed further in Chapter 5.

Since policy strategy can channel the developmental process of rental stocks, and since policy strategy will, in turn, be affected by wider power relationships in society, it follows that the manner in which rental market structuring will take place cannot be predicted. Any assumption that all rental systems are fundamentally alike and can be described and delineated by means of one uniform – and only marginally varying – process must, therefore, be treated with great suspicion.

I therefore wish to argue that the result of long-term politico-economic interaction is the emergence of rental markets which have developed in distinctive ways and which constitute contrasting models. The policy constructivist perspective leads us to look for, and attempt to explain, important divergences between the rental systems of different countries. Policy constructivism therefore focuses on the process of divergence and differentiation which results in the emergence and consolidation of alternative pathways for the development of rental housing.

The key dimension in this process is whether renting is segmented into compartmentalised and segregated markets or not. A policy strategy that reinforces differences between forms of rental provision can begin to crystallise different forms of rental provision (such as private and public renting) into mutually exclusive sub-sectors. Policy constructivism therefore does not make any assumptions that different forms of rental housing provision will necessarily crystallise into different forms of tenure. Rather, different forms of provision may either diverge or converge with each other as a result of different policy strategies being adopted.

Eventually, if the policy strategy is consistent over extended periods of time, these sub-sectors become transformed into different forms of tenure constituting mutually exclusive markets. Alternatively, a policy strategy that reduces differences between distinct forms of rental provision can result in the emergence of one integrated rental market.

Therefore, in terms of rental tenure – which itself is only one aspect of rental systems – two polar opposite alternatives are possible. On the one hand, different forms of rental provision may become increasingly polarised and ultimately transformed into different forms of tenure. On the other hand, different forms of rental provision may be harmonised and integrated to produce one form of rental tenure in which only minimal differences in provision exist between different forms of ownership and provision. The resulting diversity of rental systems among modern societies is a product of the way in which structural change in rental systems interplays with varying policy strategies designed to manage and direct such change.

I conclude from this that the decline of renting and the preference for owner occupation, where such exists, is not the inevitable outcome of either a particular configuration of power in society (such as capitalism), nor the manifestation of a natural law of demand (such as ontological security). Rather, it is socially constructed through strategic policy making as a response to the changing economic structure of rental housing stocks. It is therefore in large part the product of the manner in which the rental system has been modified by over-arching policy strategies pursued with at least some degree of consistency over extended periods of time measured in decades and generations rather than in years.

My argument does not deny the existence of exogenous factors determining the balance between renting and owning. Indeed, power relationships in the wider society between different vested rental market interests are of central importance in determining which policy strategy is likely to gain ascendancy. Nor does it question the justifiable critique made of the over-concentration in much housing research on detailed policy analysis, which, in terms of the structuring of rental markets over historically significant periods of time, must be largely dismissed as minutiae.

My concern, therefore, is to rehabilitate the significance of long-term public policy as a central determining feature of the nature of rental markets. I do so without in any way disagreeing with recent arguments about the need to get away from the narrow and short-term policy focus of traditional housing research and its fixation on tenure effects. For there is a distinct danger that the critique of the politics of tenure will lead to an over-reaction in which the significance of public policy strategy (as distinct from what might be termed the micropolitics of specific short-term tenure policies) is lost and a paralysing form of structural determinism gains analytical ascendancy.

An important part of a policy constructivist perspective must be to relate policy strategy to groupings of power between vested interests in housing and how these articulate with policy strategy formulation. Power structures therefore become vital elements in understanding the emergence, sustenance and transformation of policy strategies.

As indicated at the start of this section, policy structuring takes place in response to a specific process of economic change that rental systems – and indeed all stocks of housing – are subjected to. It is now necessary to consider this aspect of rental housing, which I term *maturation*.

THE MATURATION PROCESS

The process of maturation[1] refers to the growing gap between the per-dwelling outstanding debt on existing stock and the average new debt per dwelling that is either built, acquired, or renovated. This gap is the result of the inflation of construction costs. Each year – with only rare exceptions – that new dwellings are constructed the difference between what it cost to build the first houses erected by the housing organisation and those currently being constructed increases. Because debt servicing comprises such a large proportion of total housing costs, over a long period – many decades – maturation reduces the cost of providing old housing to well below those which result from new construction.

It should be noted that the concept of maturation is here used in a very specific sense to refer to the declining real value of the outstanding debt on a stock of dwellings. I therefore do not refer to a 'mature dwelling' but rather to a dwelling with a low outstanding debt on it, and to a stock comprising a large number of such dwellings as a mature stock of dwellings. Maturation, then, refers, in the sense meant here, to the decline in the real value of the debt of a stock of dwellings as measured by the growing differential between the average outstanding debt per dwelling for a given stock of dwellings expressed as a percentage of the value of outstanding debt per newly acquired or renovated dwelling.

Maturation is a phenomenon common to all stocks of housing, including owner occupied and profit rental housing. A mature owner occupied stock would be one in which there is a large proportion of debt-free and low-debt housing. However, first time buyers have to pay prices for old houses that commonly far exceed their original construction costs. They also commonly finance such purchases with new loans. Because of these factors, relatively mature owner occupied stocks tend to display much lower levels of maturity than cost rental stocks possessing a similar age structure. This is exacerbated by the phenomenon of mortgaging dwellings as a means of financing non-housing consumption.

In owner occupation households first entering the tenure generally buy at market prices but then individually benefit from maturation from that point on. Maturation causes severe market distortions in owner occupation because the 'rent' on housing for older debt-free households is so low that demand for housing space among this group is very inelastic, thereby encouraging high levels of consumption.

In private renting with unregulated rents, a mature housing stock enables landlords to charge rents which earn them the equivalent of a market return on the capital value of the property over and above covering actual incurred costs. The maturation process in profit renting has little relevance to demand simply because rent levels are not affected. The landlord and not the tenants benefits from the maturation process.

In cost renting, maturation impacts in different ways depending on what kind of rent-setting system is in use. Where individual historic costs determine rents a mature housing stock will mean that rents will show a declining gradient from new to old unmodernised dwellings. Rents will be high for the small proportion of tenants of new dwellings and low for the great proportion of tenants of unmodernised older dwellings possessing low levels of outstanding debt.

The life-cycle rent burden on householders of such a housing stock begins with high rents for those in new housing but falls in real terms as the dwelling ages. Both this system and owner occupation skew demand towards the older low-debt dwellings, and thereby aggravate shortages for new households by skewing the distribution of housing space and standard.

Where rent pooling is in effect, maturation will be manifest in a considerably reduced overall level of rents compared to private renting, and where rent pooling is demand-sensitive, rent levels will 'shadow' those of a profit rental market though at considerably – and sometimes drastically – lower levels. In such a system, rents will not reflect the age of the dwelling but its relative attractiveness. Housing in greater demand may have rents which produce a considerable surplus, while housing in low demand may have rents considerably below actual costs. Cross pooling is therefore used to redistribute use values to match demand.

In a rental stock subjected to rent pooling the impact of maturation is diluted. The process of maturation will only impact gradually and imperceptibly at first, becoming more evident only after maturation has reached a relatively advanced stage. This is a process which may take many decades to become evident. It is exacerbated by the fact that much cost rental housing is financed with long loans – fifty years or more – in order to keep monthly costs as low as possible. A stock of cost rental housing will therefore have a smaller proportion of debt-free dwellings than in owner occupation where loans tend to be shorter-term to enable amortisation to take place during the active working life of the buyer.

Rental systems in which profit renting and cost renting are allowed to compete with one another for tenants may result in a mixed rental market in which the rents charged by profit landlords are kept dampened by competition from cost rental housing. This possibility, as we shall see, constitutes an important policy strategy for developing a single-tenure, integrated, rental market.

The preceding description of the principle of maturation equates maturation with the inflating cost of adding to a stock of dwellings. The more rapidly the cost of acquiring new dwellings rises, the more rapidly the existing stock of dwellings can be said to mature.

It follows from this that the degree of maturation of a stock of dwellings can be measured in terms of the ratio between the average debt per existing dwelling and the average debt per newly acquired dwelling. Where that ratio is 1:1 the stock of dwellings manifests no maturation at all. That is, the average outstanding debt on the stock of dwellings is identical to the average debt on newly acquired dwellings. A ratio of 1:2 means that the average outstanding debt per existing dwelling is half that of the average debt on newly acquired dwellings and therefore indicates a degree of maturation. Ratios of 1:4 or more indicate even greater degrees of maturation. I term this measure the *maturation index*. The maturation index is higher the higher the ratio of new to existing debt is.

To give a simple example, supposing that the first batch of housing acquired by a housing co-operative cost, say, £5,000 per unit in 1970, and that the average outstanding debt on the whole stock built up to, but excluding, this year was £25,000 per dwelling. This would include both the very cheap housing of earlier years and the more expensive housing of recent years. If the current year's acquisitions cost £50,000 per dwelling then the ratio of outstanding debt to newly acquired debt in that year – the maturation index – would be 1:2. This provides a basic measure of the maturation of the housing stock.

Maturation is not simply a product of inflation, but is more complexly affected by a range of other economic factors and policy measures. An important factor is the rate at which new dwellings are added to the stock. Adding newly acquired dwellings (if, as is normally the case, they are paid for at market prices) to the existing stock reduces the average age of the total stock and increases the average debt-load per dwelling. This is termed 'front loading'. The rate at which new dwellings are added therefore affects the degree of maturation of the stock.

Periods of heavy front loading will raise the average debt per dwelling thereby decelerating the process of maturation. If front loading is sufficiently heavy for a sufficiently long period of time, the average debt per dwelling may rise to near 100 per cent of the debt per new dwelling. On the other hand, periods of light front loading will increase the average debt per dwelling only very marginally and therefore accelerate the maturation process. The interplay between rates of house price inflation and levels of investment over time in new acquisitions constitutes a rough measure of the extent of maturation.

However, the degree of maturation of a stock of dwellings can change independently of rates of new acquisitions and annual inflation in the cost of new acquisitions. Thus, for example, quite apart from new acquisitions, the process of maturation can be slowed down or even reversed by investments made either to modernise older dwellings or to carry out extraordinary programmes of repairs (such as after a war), or when dwellings are demolished.

Thus, a stock of dwellings may have high levels of maturation which are due to the extreme neglect of reinvestment in modernisation and repair. This is common in private renting and to some extent in owner occupation, particularly where the owner occupied market has a large number of marginal low-income buyers or elderly households.

Other influences on maturation include the extent of equity leakage. Thus, the sale of low-debt dwellings where the capital receipts are not fully reinvested in new acquisitions may reverse the maturation process, raising average debt-loads in the existing stock.

This happens in owner occupation when dwellings are either sold or re-mortgaged and all or part of the proceeds are either consumed or invested outside the housing market. Equity removed by the selling household is often replaced with debt raised by the buying household.

This also happens in public renting when dwellings are sold at discounted prices. The discount, pocketed by the buying tenant, represents the difference between the amount received from the sale and the sum needed to buy a replacement dwelling. Equity removed by the buying household in the form of a discount is replaced with new loans on new acquisitions raised by the public housing organisation.

The effect in public renting is an increase in the average outstanding debt per dwelling of the remaining unsold stock and a passing on of higher housing costs to the remaining tenants who do not buy. This equity leakage in public renting is often masked because receipts can still be sufficient to pay off more debt than was on the dwelling sold, particularly if the dwelling sold was an old one and front loading is very low. It may therefore seem as though the sale has benefited remaining tenants. Yet if we compare the post-sale maturation index with what the maturation index would have been had the sale been at market price it will be clear that maturation has been retarded in relative terms.

The process of maturation may therefore be highly variable. Its trajectory will also vary in relation to a range of different factors, including the extent of front loading and the rate of inflation both in the cost of newbuild and in incomes. It is for this reason that maturation reflects a range of factors including the social composition of households occupying the housing stock, how tax incentives or dis-incentives influence investment, public policy towards public renting, and rental management strategies.

The phenomenon of maturation has been greatly neglected in the literature on public renting. There are a number of reasons for this. The main one is probably that for much of the post-war period, at least until the late 1960s, public renting has remained relatively immature and so maturation has not played a major role in determining cost structures. This has been accentuated by the fact that until fairly recently public subsidies to public renting have often been consider-able – at least as much as to owner occupation and sometimes more – and this has focused attention on the impact of subsidies at the expense of the maturation process on keeping rents low.

Another reason is that economic theory does not recognise historic costs as a sufficient measure of costs. In terms of accounting the difference between the price paid for a dwelling and current market value is treated as capital that needs to earn interest at going rates in order to cover costs. Working out 'costs' in owner occupation is normally done by the occupiers themselves. They use a common-sense approach which tells them that as their debt falls in real terms their costs decline. They do not consider the capital value of the difference between outstanding debt and market price as capital which could be earning interest if the dwelling were sold. In working out the 'costs' of a cost rental stock, by contrast, economists and accountants commonly do set off the lost interest as a foregone income. This has led to the peculiar – but important – consequence that most ordinary people are fully aware of the benefits of historic costs in owner occupation but not in public renting.

Another factor is that the phenomenon of maturation is little understood because it has been little analysed. It is therefore possible to argue that maturation is only very marginal in reducing costs because modernisation and major periodic renovation effectively evens out the debt-loads of old and new dwellings.

This is in fact an empirical question. As we shall see when we examine actual cases later in the book, the maturation index can be very high: 1:5 or more. The evidence is therefore that matura-tion does in fact play a major part in reducing the rents of cost rental housing.

Finally, we may note that there are good ideological and political reasons why those who wish to retain public renting as a disadvan-taged and restricted form of housing would understandably wish to divert attention from the extent to which historic costs keep rents low and focus instead on subsidies as the reason for low rents. The neglect of maturation in cost renting and the widespread ignorance about its importance in keeping rents low is ideologically important in minimising the political support for cost renting. This brings me to the policy dimension of the maturation process.

COST RENTING, MATURATION AND POLICY STRATEGY

It is the maturation of cost renting and the manner in which policy making both influences maturation and is a response to maturation that is of central interest in this discussion. We have noted that the maturation process for cost rental tenants tends to be slower than for individual owner occupiers. This is due to longer average loan terms and because rent pooling, where it is employed, tends to dampen the decline in real costs accruing to individual tenants because the imputed rental income generated by maturation is averaged across the whole stock.

For historical reasons, cost renting has also tended to be considerably less mature than profit renting, and will continue to be so for at least several more decades. This is mainly because profit renting is an older form of rental provision manifesting high levels of maturity in contrast to public renting and cost renting which in many countries are an almost purely post-1945 phenomenon.

But it is also because profit rental housing is less commonly provided by means of 100 per cent loans than is public renting, and because – under some policy regimes at least – there is a greater tendency for profit landlords to neglect investment in maintenance and modernisation in order to maximise short-term profits.

Despite these considerable differences, however, sooner or later the course of the maturation process in cost renting reaches a point at which debt-servicing falls in real terms to a level at which cost renting begins to compete strongly with other forms of housing, particularly profit renting, tenant ownership and owner occupation. This is reflected in falling real rents and lengthening waiting lists for cost rental housing which in turn build up pressure for some policy response.

The process of maturation – once it reaches the point at which cost rents fall substantially below private market rents – therefore calls for fundamental policy decisions to be made. These concern the whole balance between the tenures, which the maturation of cost renting threatens to upset. Most importantly, the continued expansion of cost renting threatens the continued expansion of owner occupation. It is important to note here that some policy response to the process of maturation in cost renting is unavoidable. Politicians must make a strategic policy decision to either increase new constructions to meet demand or to undermine maturation by adopting a range of containment and destabilisation measures.

Increasing new constructions will encourage cost renting to expand and so cater for wider and wider groups of households by building or acquiring more housing to shorten waiting lists. As maturation progresses this pressure grows rather than lessens, until cost renting begins to squeeze out demand for owner occupation. The other alternative is therefore to counteract the benefits of maturation, for example by charging surplus generating rents that are then siphoned off as a form of implicit taxation, or reducing access to the stock by reducing its size through a programme of heavily discounted sales.

The third alternative of simply not doing anything, and allowing the pressure of demand to continue to build up as maturation continues to increase is untenable in the long run because increasingly high levels of unsatisfied demand are politically problematic. The process of maturation will therefore sooner or later reach a point at which decisions about the future direction of the development of cost renting must be faced.

We will now consider the major policy strategies that may be developed to channel the maturation process of cost rental housing.

4 Reconceptualising rental systems

POLICY STRATEGIES TOWARDS COST RENTING

Encouraging cost renting to expand or suppressing it (by either counteracting the maturation process or withdrawing its benefits from tenants) amount to two principal and opposing ways of treating cost renting. We will see in Part II when we look at concrete examples that this is a very crude over-simplification, and a more nuanced model of policy constructivist strategies will be developed later. For now, we may consider the two polar types of strategy towards cost renting – encouraging and suppressing – in their broadest and simplest outline.

Encouraging cost renting involves allowing it to continue to expand and to use its high level of maturation to compete with profit renting. This leads to a dampening of rent levels and possibly in the long run to eliminating profit renting through competition. I term the market that this results in an *integrated rental market* or a *unitary rental market*.

There are two reasons for adopting this terminology. In the first place the policy strategy aims to integrate different forms of rental provision by minimising differences between them. The strategy therefore leads to increasing integration and homogeneity between profit orientated and non-profit-orientated rental housing. Secondly, integration is sought by relying on market mechanisms. Cost renting is sheltered from competition by rent regulation only until such time as it attains a sufficient degree of maturation to enable it to compete with profit renting on more or less equal terms. The ultimate goal is therefore to create a rental system in which different forms of rental provision compete in a market on broadly similar terms.

Unitary rental markets are a classic example of the social market philosophy in operation. The aim is to keep the profit motive as an element in rental markets but to ameliorate it as much as possible by encouraging non-profit forms of rental housing. The result is a mixed market in which social and economic considerations both play a part in determining the supply and demand of housing.

Suppressing cost renting, by contrast, involves ghettoising it into a public rental sector that comprises a strictly controlled minority form of housing on which surplus-generating rents are charged and from which the better-off tenants are encouraged to leave: a phenomenon commonly referred to as residualisation. It is simultaneously suppressed in order to undermine its maturity, commonly by compelling cost rental organisations to sell dwellings with large – and often enormous – discounts: 60, 70, even 90 per cent are not uncommon in some countries.

I term the rental system that results from this a *dualist rental system* since its distinguishing characteristic is the existence of parallel public and private rental systems subject to increasingly divergent forms of provision and conditions of tenure. When such divergence is highly developed, different forms of provision can ultimately harden into different forms of tenure. Furthermore, unlike a unitary rental market, dualist rental systems do not depend on competition and so do not constitute a market. Rather, they comprise two separate systems: one more or less unregulated private rental market and a public means-tested allocation system.

The adoption of a discernible strategy at a particular point in time I term a *historic juncture*. This is a juncture between on the one hand a growing gap between rent levels in profit renting and cost renting and on the other hand the emergence and implementation of a policy constructivist response to influence the organisation of the rental system in a given direction.

The widening of rent differentials between profit and cost renting can be – and often is – the result of other processes than the maturation of cost renting. It can, for example, be the result of the removal of rent controls on profit renting, as happened in Britain in the 1960s, or the result of a period of heavy subsidisation and blanket rent control of cost renting, as happened in New Zealand during the 1940s.

However, even in such cases, maturation plays a definite role as a deeper long-term underlying factor in sustaining or increasing rent differentials. Thus, as we shall see in the cases presented below, in Britain, the removal of rent controls on private renting during the 1960s would not have created wide rent differentials if council housing had not attained an advanced state of maturation. In the New

Zealand case, heavy subsidisation combined with rapid house price increases in the 1940s conjoined to aggravate rent differentials.

The dualist model

For those who wish to discourage cost renting, its maturation is a 'problem' since the decline in real rent levels that is the result of the maturation process increases demand for cost renting in the form of long waiting lists. This places pressure on policy makers to either increase the supply of cost rental housing in order to satisfy the growing demand, or to dampen demand both by making cost renting less attractive and by reducing its availability.

The process of maturation therefore provides the conditions in which considerable pressure exists for governments to make a strategic policy decision over the future of cost renting. For governments that wish to restrict the role of cost renting, the process of maturation constitutes a challenge to formulate policies to cope with the problems that the maturation process brings about.

It is therefore possible to describe these circumstances as a *rent-differential crisis* in which policies are deemed necessary to undermine the maturation process in order to contain cost renting in a residual role. A rent-differential crisis emerges when differences in the rents of cost and profit renting become so great as to call forth a government response.

I term the policy towards cost renting that results from adopting a dualist strategy a *command policy* because the underlying policy strategy is to hive off cost renting into a state regulated rental sub-sector that is subject to increasingly divergent forms of provision from profit renting. This involves increasing centralised political control over the cost rental sector in order to residualise it by a variety of measures and thereafter to keep it residualised. The process of increasing centralised political control over cost renting leads to the establishment of a command economy in public renting.

Measures to residualise cost renting can be divided into those aimed at dampening demand and those aimed at reducing supply. Of course, reducing the supply of cost rental housing also indirectly reduces demand as the harder it is to obtain such housing the greater the proportion of ordinary households who will be deterred from even seeking it and who will therefore be effectively steered towards other forms of housing.

The most direct way to reduce demand in a rapidly maturing cost rental sector is to raise rents as near to market levels as possible. This has the additional advantage of generating public income. Equally important, compelling cost rental organisations to charge surplus-generating rents that supplement local or central taxation revenues also encourages as many tenants as possible to leave. If this is combined with a highly selective and targeted housing allowance system, it further reduces demand.

On the supply side, setting very low ceilings on borrowing for newbuild and renovation restricts supply. This also keeps housing standards low, since under-investment leads to the neglect of repairs and maintenance and of renovation programmes. This, however, is a long-term measure that needs to be sustained over decades to have a noticeable cumulative effect.

Of course, some withdrawal of finance for renovation must be understood as a short-term economy measure. However, when this is kept up for years or even decades it becomes increasingly difficult to explain away in these terms. Behind the systematic and long-term deprivation of investment for renovation and modernisation lies an essentially 'poorhouse' attitude to public renting: that it is for the most marginalised households only, that they should be grateful for whatever housing they are offered, and that it should not be too attractive.

A much faster way of reducing supply is through forcible asset stripping by means of central government legislated compulsory sales at heavily discounted (i.e. market-subverting) prices. Discounts are effectively subsidies to tenants in order to induce them to buy. Discounted sales decrease the asset value of the remaining stock. But the main impact of discounted sales is to reduce the total size of the stock, restricting the scale of re-lets and thereby limiting access.

The elegance of this measure is that the size of discount can be varied between households in order to selectively decimate the stock. This may be done, for example, by giving greater discounts to those who have held longer tenancies. By this means, older low-debt properties can be sold off to reduce the average age of the remaining unsold stock and thereby induce a degree of maturation reversal.

Such measures require a considerable degree of central government control in order to implement. Cost rental organisations are commonly unwilling to either charge surplus-generating rents or to asset strip. Central government therefore normally has to intervene to compel measures such as these. In so intervening they must ensure that all possible loopholes that could be exploited by the cost rental housing organisations are closed. This in turn demands the continual monitoring of the impact of central government measures and often a progressive shift of strategic management decision making from the local managing organisation to central government.

Typical for command policies is therefore the political management of cost rental housing at the highest levels of government, often as high as ministerial or even cabinet level. Rent setting, determining levels of investment in newbuild and renovation, determining policy towards the sale of cost rental housing and other key strategic managerial decisions that need to be taken at regular intervals – annually or even more frequently – are typically increasingly concentrated into the hands of senior central government politicians. Cost renting is thereby gradually transmogrified into public renting with an increasingly intimate relationship between the economy of cost rental housing and the exercise of centralised political power.

The parallel between command policies towards cost renting and the working of state socialist command economies is too striking to overlook. It is also notable that the net results are very similar, in that the system produces chronic shortages and market insensitivity. Thus, for example, the politicisation of investment decisions that characterises command policies produces chronic under-investment in cost renting that parallels those that characterise state socialist command economies in general.

The major difference between them in this respect is, however, that chronic under-investment and asset stripping in command policies are clearly – and sometimes explicitly – designed to undermine the economy of cost renting and thereby to residualise it, whereas in state socialist command economies this is an unintended result.

Command policies towards cost renting are commonly intended as one of a number of measures to force the home ownership rate as high as possible. We have noted in an earlier chapter that in most cases, the prime motivation for setting up a state-run cost rental sector in the first place was to provide a safety net to the private rental market. But by the time a historic juncture occurs it is only a secondary purpose to shelter the private rental market from cost rental competition. Dualist rental systems primarily prevent the emergence of a rental market that might tempt large numbers of households to continue renting rather than buy into owner occupation.

Such a strategy has far-reaching consequences. In social terms, residualisation involves narrowing the social basis of households comprising both rental sectors to largely temporary private renters and, in the public rental sector, to long-term rental households that are unable (or despite the heavy loading of the political dice in favour of buying, are unwilling) to buy rather than to rent housing.

The dualist strategy also has implications for how government manages the owner occupied sector. Suppressing cost renting compels more and more households who are denied access to cost renting into attempting to enter owner occupation. As a direct result of the policy of the suppression of cost renting, therefore, political pressure is created for escalating subsidies to owner occupiers to bring ever more marginal households into owner occupation, in what I have termed in the Australian context *the ratchet effect* (Kemeny, 1983a, pp. 104–5).

In Kemeny (1983a) I argued that the ratchet effect was caused by the increasing gap between the heavily subsidised owner occupiers and unsubsidised – or increasingly the negatively subsidised – public tenants. This in turn puts political pressure on governments to increase access to owner occupation by increasing subsidies to potential marginal buyers.

I argued that the growing gap between subsidies to owners and renters raises levels of experienced relative deprivation among that group of renters which could buy if they were in receipt of larger subsidies. Extending subsidies to this group reduces the size of the non-owning rump of renters, but because the now reduced rump comprises poorer and more marginal households than the preceding larger rump, the cost of a further tightening of the ratchet to bring the same number of these within the ranks of the subsidised buyers is considerably increased.

This argument needs to be complemented by the crucial factor that it is the deliberately created shortage of cost rental housing that impels more and more households to buy who would not do so if cost rental housing were in adequate supply. The motivation for suppressing cost renting is to force as many households as possible to choose between profit renting and owner occupation by denying them access to cost renting. For most households, especially those with children, this is a Hobson's choice. So the smaller the cost rental sector the larger will be the proportion of low-income households effectively forced to buy to obtain housing that both provides security of tenure and is at least approximately cost covering.

It therefore takes progressively larger and larger subsidies to bring about progressively smaller and smaller decreases in the ever more marginalised and impoverished rump of non-buyers. One of the hallmarks of a dualist strategy is therefore a shift in subsidies from all owner occupiers to marginal owners and marginal first-time buyers: a shift that is now beginning to take place in Britain. But while each increase in subsidies to marginal owner occupiers draws a few more economically marginal households precariously into the privileged tenure, the gap grows between the subsidy 'haves' and the rump of the subsidy 'have-nots', which further increases pressure for further subsidies.

We might also note here that one consequence of the ratchet effect is that the growing proportion of marginal buyers in the owner occupied sector creates increasing instability in the owner occupied housing market. With high proportions of marginal buyers in the tenure owner occupation becomes more sensitive to economic boom–slump cycles in the form of more acute glut–famine housing cycles, higher rates of mortgage default during economic downturns, and in some countries (notably the USA, but increasingly also in Britain) abandonment. The tendency is therefore for the glut–famine cycles in owner occupation to have higher peaks and deeper troughs as the proportion of low-income earners in the tenure increases. I term this effect *glut–famine amplification*.

The English experience, since the rapid increase in the home ownership rate during the 1980s is a particularly striking example of glut–famine amplification and the resultant increasing instability in the owner occupied housing market. Glut–famine housing cycles have been becoming more extreme since the first major famine of the late 1960s when the home ownership rate passed the 50 per cent mark. By the late 1980s when the home ownership rate passed 65 per cent, the famine at that time and the equally great glut that followed it in the early 1990s were much more acute and prolonged than earlier cycles had been.

The ratchet effect also impacts upon the nature of private profit-orientated landlordism. The emergence of a low-income owner occupier sector encourages the expansion of a form of petty landlordism that I have described elsewhere as *owner occupier* (or *petty*) *landlordism* (Kemeny, 1981a, pp. 79–85). As more tenants with lower incomes are encouraged into owner occupation, private renting becomes increasingly dominated by owner occupiers renting out their homes for short periods (for example when unable to sell during a glut, or while temporarily away) or renting rooms in their homes to eke out either low incomes heavily committed to high mortgage repayments or low pensions. This phenomenon was already noticed by Rex and Moore (1967) in inner-city areas during the 1960s. A feature of such landlordism is also that since these landlords are renting out their main home or a part of it, they are centrally concerned both to select tenants carefully and to deny them security of tenure.

The ratchet effect is particularly evident once the owner occupation rate has been forced up to approaching or even exceeding two-thirds of households. At that point the owner occupied sector has become swollen by sufficient marginal buyers to create a noticeable ratchet effect. It is at this point, too, that subsidies to owner occupation begin noticeably to shift from general ones to subsidies focused on marginal first-time buyers and mortgage defaulters.

The type of rental system that the dualist rental strategy results in is that which exists in English-speaking countries (Britain, and particularly England; Ireland; the USA; Canada; Australia; and New Zealand). It is also found in a number of other countries, notably Iceland (Sveinsson, 1993) and Finland (Ruonavaara, 1987).

Access to the public rental sector in a dualist rental system is severely limited, effectively to a decreasing proportion of those who are in extreme and urgent need of housing. Public rents are kept high, partly as a result of much older and low-debt housing being sold into owner occupation at a discount thereby reversing the maturation process. More importantly, much, or even all, of rent rebates to poor tenants are paid for from the high rents of better-off tenants (made possible by the high degree of maturation of the public rental stock) in preference to being paid from social security.

This suppression of maturation is sustained by regular intervention by central government to ensure rents are raised, to limit public rental borrowing by restricting the re-mortgaging of debt-free housing assets, and to adjust the size of discounts for purchasing tenants to keep the sale of public rental housing at high levels. Private renting is left as unregulated as possible and generally unsubsidised. Owner occupation is encouraged by generous subsidies which increasingly shift from all owner occupiers to marginal buyers.

The unitary model

The alternative strategy to suppressing cost renting is to take advantage of maturation by allowing cost renting to compete with profit renting and owner occupation, thereby creating an integrated or unitary rental market. In such a market the maturation of cost renting is used to exert downward market pressure on profit rents in order to limit landlord profit extraction from rental housing.

This is made possible because the maturation of cost renting enables cost rental housing organisations to undercut profit renting. Once cost rental organisations gain a significant share of the rental market they act as market leaders, determining the maximum level of private rents by their market preponderance.

In the long run, cost rental housing is likely to eliminate or at least severely restrict profit renting. Equally important, it provides a realistic rental alternative to owner occupation by making it attractive for a significant proportion of households to remain in the rental market. However, considerable profits may be possible in the profit-orientated rental stock until such time as cost rental organisations have built up a stock of housing that is fully mature and comprises a sufficiently large proportion of rental housing in all geographical and socio-economic sectors of the market.

Unitary rental markets may therefore range from being purely cost rental in nature (a *unitary cost rental market*), to manifesting various degrees of profit extraction (a *unitary part-profit rental market*). However, a *unitary profit rental market* is unlikely to ever be feasible, even though in theory cost rental housing could be converted into profit rental housing (for example by floating cost rental housing companies on the stock exchange). This is simply because the high rents that would result would create the need to provide some form of cheap rental housing for low-income earners. The result of this would be that having abolished cost renting, governments would then be forced to reinvent it and develop a new restricted access means-tested public rental sector. The dualist system would thereby be reasserted.

Unitary cost rental markets will have cost rental housing which has attained a high degree of maturity and comprise a substantial proportion of the total rental market. Maturity results in rent levels highly competitive with owner occupation and creates a heavy demand for rental housing. This in turn creates a large and expanding rental sector that offers a genuine alternative to owner occupation. Such a rental market serves households from all socio-economic groups that have actively chosen to rent.

Unitary rental markets in which cost rental housing is less mature and comprises a smaller percentage of the total rental housing stock will take the form of a unitary part-profit rental market in which rents will be somewhat higher than in a unitary cost rental market. This will be because the cost rental stock is not large enough to strongly influence rent levels on the rental market as a whole and/or its maturity is insufficient to significantly undercut private rents.

However, in the medium run the process of maturation will – assuming policy allows this to continue – enable the cost rental organisations to increasingly whittle away at private rent levels and move the rental system towards a unitary cost rental market. In this strategy, maturation is not a problem but an opportunity. It makes possible the phasing out of both rent regulation and subsidies to enable cost renting to increasingly compete with profit renting on equal terms in a deregulated and integrated rental market.

However, the timing of the harmonisation of public and private rents will be the central factor in determining the extent to which profit extraction by private landlords will take place. If harmonisation takes place before cost renting has attained a high degree of maturation, profit extraction will be relatively high and may continue for several decades. If, however, harmonisation is postponed by delaying the phasing in of rent deregulation while waiting for full maturation to be attained, the ensuing 'market non-conforming' rent control measures necessary to prevent high levels of private profit extraction will distort demand and place strains on the policy. This in turn may increase opposition to the unitary rental market policy with calls for its abandonment by freeing private rents and residualising cost renting.

In contrast to the creation of a dualist system, then, a unitary rental market policy does not face a rent-differential crisis but rather an often long – but essentially transitional – *harmonisation problematic*. During this time, rent regulation is gradually eased such that the rent-setting system becomes increasingly market conforming. The central problematic of such a policy is therefore to time the movement towards the complete deregulation of both cost rents and the rents of profit-orientated landlords, while avoiding the Scylla of market distortion and the Charybdis of profit extraction.

I term the policy response deriving from such a strategy a *market policy*, since it is based on letting cost rental housing organisations move towards free and unregulated competition with private renting and phasing out state control over rent setting. Examples of countries which have been moving towards a unitary rental market – albeit in different ways – include Sweden, The Netherlands, Germany, Switzerland, Austria and Denmark. However, as we shall see later, the market policies of at least the first four of these countries differ significantly from one another in important respects.

DUALIST AND UNITARY SYSTEMS COMPARED

The prime differences between dualist and unitary systems can be summarised as follows:

1 In a dualist system cost renting is provided in the form of a state controlled public housing sector run as a command economy, while in a unitary market cost rental housing organisations

compete with private landlords for households under increasingly deregulated conditions.

2 In a dualist system private profit renting is left largely to sink or swim, while in a unitary market it is supported often on equal or nearly equal terms to cost renting.

3 In a dualist system, owner occupation is given favoured-tenure status, while in a unitary market tenure neutrality is a principal aim.

The overall result is to produce radically different housing systems. This is most striking in the share of the total stock of housing going to different forms of tenure and different forms of rental provision. Table 1 is extracted from Power (1993), and, showing two countries identified in this discussion as dualist and two countries identified as unitary, illustrates this point well.

Table 1 Patterns of owner occupation and renting in dualist and unitary rental systems (%)

	Owner occupation	Private renting	Cost renting	Public renting	Total
Dualist					
UK	66	7	3	24	100
Ireland	78	9	0.5	13	100
Unitary					
Denmark	58	21	18	3	100
Germany	37	38	25	0	100

Source: Power (1993) p. 10, Table 1.1.

As we shall see when we examine specific countries in more detail, similar patterns to those found in the above dualist and unitary rental systems are found elsewhere. Sweden has an owner occupier sector of 40 per cent, a private rental sector of 20 per cent and a cost rental sector of 23 per cent,[1] and both Australia and New Zealand have large owner occupied sectors but, like the UK and Ireland, have little or no cost renting.[2]

However, these patterns are only indicative. The central difference between the countries is whether the different forms of rental provision are integrated, or in the process of being integrated, into a single rental market. From this follows the general pattern of tenures in Table 1, though with substantial variations.

The two types of rental systems – dualist and unitary – together with their respective policy strategies – command and market – constitute broad conceptual categories. Within these, considerable variations may be found from country to country. These depend not just on which overall rental strategy has been pursued but on a variety of other factors. They include levels of maturation, the varying roles of cost rental housing, different systems of subsidy, and at what particular points in time in the maturation process historic junctures have occurred to change courses of development.

There is also a clear cultural dimension. As we have already noted, the English-speaking countries have in many ways provided the basic model of the dualist rental system command policy. But the countries that have opted for unitary rental markets also constitute a cultural block, though one centred both geographically and culturally on Germany.

This is not a coincidence as many aspects of German social structure – notably the non-adversarial legal system and education – particularly the gymnasium and, in higher education, public doctoral disputations and the docentship system – have also been adopted by countries with unitary rental market policies. In addition, and more important as a potential explanatory factor, these countries possess similarities in their internal power structures, with corporatism being a major characteristic of the structure of power and decision making.

5 Power, ideology and rental market policy structuring

INTRODUCTION

Although this study is primarily concerned with analysing the mechanisms of change in rental markets and outlining the principal and contrasting models of rental markets that have developed among industrialised countries, a second and equally vital issue is why these differences have emerged. Describing them in cultural terms – anglo-saxon and germanic models – is useful as an initial classification, but is not an explanation.

The influence of the ordo-liberals in the post-war construction of West Germany must have been based on an existing power structure and associated political processes, however minimal this may have been in the ruins of the war. There is therefore likely to be some underlying feature of the social and political structure of the countries involved that results in the tendency for policy constructivism to produce such different rental market outcomes.

The solution must be sought, I believe, in the different power structures and political organisation that these two groups of countries possess. English-speaking countries are essentially two-party states, while the germanic block of countries are characterised by a more corporatist type of political organisation, often involving multiple political parties, coalition governments, and the representation of a wide range of interests in political and policy compromises. The explanation for the emergence of dualist rental systems in English-speaking countries and the development of unitary rental markets in the germanic block of countries may well be found in the manner in which the emergence of a given policy strategy is influenced by different expressions of the exercise of power.

Before tackling this question directly, I examine Esping-Andersen's (1990) explanation of the differences between welfare states. This study has evoked considerable interest and represents one of the more ambitious attempts to explain different types of welfare states. It does so in terms of power structures and therefore provides a useful general introduction to the wider issues behind the emergence of different rental systems.

This discussion is also intended to point up the importance of not treating rental systems in isolation from other social policy areas and from the wider context of the organisation of the welfare state. Rental systems are only one dimension of housing systems, which, in turn, represent only one – albeit major – area of social policy in the construction of welfare states. If we are to understand why rental systems differ so fundamentally from one another then it is important that we attempt to understand those differences in the wider policy constructivist context of the welfare state as a whole.

THREE WORLDS OF CAPITALISM AND TWO WORLDS OF RENTING?

Comparative analysis of welfare states has become much more conceptually and theoretically aware in the last decade or so (Kemeny, 1992a, Ch. 5). One of the most ambitious attempts to distinguish between welfare regimes has been Esping-Andersen (1990). He argued that three distinct types could be identified. One type was what he terms *liberal*, characterised by minimum welfare provision for the poorest members of society. The liberal regime is represented by what he calls the anglo-saxon countries, and particularly the newer settler countries. Another type, made up of a large group of countries, he identifies as *corporatist* in which welfare provision is stratified along the lines of major interest cleavages (such as class, occupation, religion and ethnicity). Corporatist regimes are represented by countries such as Germany, France, Austria and The Netherlands. Finally, he identifies a small group of countries which possess what he terms a *social democratic* regime, embodying principles of universalism and comprehensive welfare provision and represented by the Scandinavian countries.

Esping-Andersen makes it quite clear that he develops an inductive model derived from allowing his complex data to speak for themselves. I will argue below that there is in fact a theoretical perspective that informs at least part of the classification. But to start with I want to consider the extent to which his threefold schema is isomorphic with my own twofold schema of rental systems.

Esping-Andersen's analysis has some features in common with the analysis of rental systems presented in this book. The most important is that the liberal anglo-saxon model of residual welfare provision described by Esping-Andersen fits very well with the command rental strategy described above. It is precisely those countries that have residual welfare provision that also tend to have dualist rental systems with residualised state-run 'command economy' type cost rental sectors.

The major possible exception, at least in terms of possessing a less extremely residualised welfare state, is Britain. Yet it is an exception that proves the rule, since though the British welfare state is still relatively well developed, it possesses strong elements of residual welfare and, most important, has been in an undeniable state of contraction and decline for decades. The period since the early 1980s, in particular, has seen a dramatic decline in welfare standards. This decline has been masked to some extent by rising social security expenditure needed to finance high levels of unemployment. There are therefore strong grounds for arguing that the British welfare system is in the process of being transformed into the liberal model represented by the anglophone settler countries.

Britain's cost rental sector is undergoing similar processes of contraction and restructuring. Despite very considerable local and regional variations, it, too, has never been envisaged – at least nationally – as anything more than a complement to the private market, albeit on a very much larger scale than in other English-speaking countries. Even Labour governments have never made any efforts to integrate public and private renting. Britain's rental sector has therefore always reflected a basically dualist strategy. And since the early 1980s it has been undergoing a very marked process of contraction and residualisation.

Esping-Andersen's second model – corporatist – is more problematic. The category is a large one, including such diverse countries as Germany, France and Italy. Because Esping-Andersen's corporatist model is derived from an inductive analysis of a large body of data, it seems to have little in common with conceptions of corporatism in the political science literature (Lehmbruch, 1984; Lijphart and Crepaz, 1991; Rothstein, 1987; Schmitter, 1982; Wilson, 1983). Nor does Esping-Andersen even refer to the corporatist literature. He therefore has nothing to say about how conceptions of corporatism in political science relate to his own schema.

This is particularly problematic because the third (and small) cluster of countries he identifies as having universal and comprehensive welfare provision includes one country – Sweden – which is commonly identified in the political science literature as the outstanding example of a corporatist society (for a discussion see Kemeny, 1992c). Indeed, in a wide-ranging secondary analysis of the corporatist literature, Lijpart and Crepaz (1991) calculate that, according to 6 leading scholars of corporatism who analysed 18 countries, Norway, Sweden and Denmark are all among the 5 countries highest ranked in this regard.

The reason for the disjunction between countries defined as corporatist by Esping-Andersen and those defined as corporatist in the political science literature on corporatist theory is probably due to the labour movement perspective – or as Esping-Andersen terms it here 'working class mobilization theory' (Esping-Andersen, 1990, pp. 105–11). Esping-Andersen has been a central figure in developing labour movement theory in his earlier work. In order to understand why Esping-Andersen excludes the Scandinavian countries from the corporatist category and puts them in a category of their own it is necessary to briefly describe the main differences between corporatist theory and labour movement theory.

Labour movement theory has been particularly well developed in Scandinavia (Esping-Andersen, 1985; Korpi, 1978, 1983) but has become generally established as an alternative to corporatist theory (Castles, 1978; Stephens, 1979; Tilton, 1990). Labour movement theory differs from corporatism in the way in which labour radicalism is viewed. According to labour movement theory, the extent to which the welfare state is developed in industrial societies is dependent on the relative strength of the labour movement and its political ability to implement collective welfare provision through electoral control of the state.

Labour movement theory therefore rejects the 'end of ideology' arguments that are implicit in some of the corporatist literature, with its assumptions of inevitable capitalist hegemony. Nor does it see the state as some sort of neutral co-ordinator of labour and capital interests in which the welfare state is a lame end product of corporatist compromise. Instead, the state is seen more as an instrument for the labour movement to gain control over for the attainment of its ends, albeit by electoral means. In this view, the welfare state is seen as one step on the road to socialism achieved through the ballot box. Labour movement theory can therefore be understood as the modern representative of conceptions of the democratic class struggle as developed by Lipset and others.

Esping-Andersen's view of corporatism as the product of class compromise contrasts with the working-class ascendancy in social democratic societies that his view of labour movement theory posits. It is therefore hard to avoid the conclusion that his welfare states typology has been developed along lines that are congruent with this distinction. So Esping-Andersen's distinction between corporatist and comprehensive welfare states reflects his more general analysis of the nature of power in industrial society.

Labour movement theory places the three Scandinavian countries of Denmark, Norway and Sweden in its own category of countries with strong labour movements that have produced strong welfare states. In taking this as a starting point, corporatist theory must necessarily be abandoned. It is hardly possible to develop a category of corporatist societies that excludes three of the societies that are commonly seen as among the most clear examples of corporatist societies in the world.

Because corporatism is a shared feature of the political systems of countries with unitary rental markets, the lack of a point of common reference between Esping-Andersen's schema and the political science literature on corporatism makes it difficult to reconcile his schema with the distinction between dualist and unitary rental systems developed in this book.

However, I want to argue that there need be no irreconcilable contradiction here. Esping-Andersen's focus on the power of the labour movement to mobilise politically does not preclude a political system of corporatism in countries with strong labour movements. On the contrary, one might usefully describe countries which have both a strong labour movement and a clearly corporatist power structure – notably Sweden, but also to some extent the other Scandinavian countries – as forms of 'labour-led' corporatism (Kemeny, 1992c). In such countries, universalist principles governing the distribution of welfare may be so well developed as to justify their definition as a distinct welfare regime.

POWER STRUCTURES AND RENTAL MARKETS

The most fruitful line of investigation to uncover the reasons why unitary rental markets emerge in some countries but not others may well be the nature of the national power structure. Corporatist theory in its classic formulation is defined as a system of co-operation and compromise between capital and labour that is orchestrated by the state.

Reality is somewhat more messy and complicated. In practice, corporatism might be best understood as a system of institutionalised political representation of different interest groups that is essentially founded on compromise and accommodation between conflicting power groupings – whether these be based on class, religion or ethnicity. Corporatist systems therefore provide an institutional framework in which a wide range of different interests can be represented in the policy-making process. Countries with predominantly two-party systems of political decision making tend to polarise interests into one of the two principal blocs, which in turn can lead to smaller interest groups being squeezed out of the policy-making process.

The suspicion that unitary rental markets tend to be found in corporatist societies, while dualist rental systems tend to be found in liberal two-party regimes is supported to a considerable degree by the findings of Lijphart and Crepaz (1991). Although this data must be treated with great caution, it provides a suggestive indication of the tendency towards corporatism among societies possessing unitary rental systems. According to this ranking, the 6 countries I have identified as possessing unitary rental markets (Austria, Denmark, Germany, The Netherlands, Sweden and Switzerland) occupy 6 of the 7 top positions in Lijphart and Crepaz's ranking of corporatist societies, while the UK plus the 4 anglophone settler societies of Australia, New Zealand, Canada[1] and the USA occupy the bottom 5 positions.

The weakness of corporatism in English-speaking countries may well explain the weak position of private landlordism in countries with dualist rental systems. As only one of a number of housing market interests, private landlords have tended to become squeezed out between the support for owner occupation in conservative political parties and the support for public renting in socialist parties.[2]

It is perhaps paradoxical to argue that dualist rental systems tend to emerge in societies with a politically weak landlord class. After all, dualist rental systems are ostensibly intended to encourage the development of a free profit rental market. It might therefore be thought that dualist systems are precisely the ones that might be expected to develop in countries with a strong landlord class.

Much the same can be said of cost rental housing organisations and self-help housing movements. These smaller interest groupings have found it difficult to find a political base in which their interests can be effectively represented. Their natural home in a two-party system might have been the country's principal socialist party. However, socialist parties have traditionally pursued a strategy of developing strong state institutions at both local and national levels.

The reason for this has much to do with the fact that socialist parties in many English-speaking countries – most notably Britain,

Australia and New Zealand – have been effectively the political wing of strong trades union movements. Labour movements in these countries have therefore tended to be divided into an industrial wing, focusing on workplace-based action such as campaigning for improving wages and conditions, and a political wing, focusing on constructing solutions to social problems based on the local and national state.

Co-operative solutions, from a very early stage, had great vitality and became important innovative movements. Workers insurance schemes, co-operative wholesale and retail societies, trustee savings banks, and a host of other co-operative and mutual aid ventures, most of them originally locally based, promised to transform society from within. However, as socialist aspirations switched from mutual aid and self-help to industrial and political reforms these movements lost their reforming zeal, and either withered on the vine or became oligarchised and virtually indistinguishable from profit-driven ventures.

Housing was one of the areas that had anyway been least developed by the early flowering of co-operation and mutual aid. The building societies in Britain and Australia were probably the most developed example of this, but like their counterparts in other spheres of activity they oligarchised and in more recent years have become little different from joint-stock banking companies. More important, there never emerged any significant cost rental or co-operative rental movement. The weak mutual aid base and profound statism that has permeated socialist party thinking has discouraged other forms of cost renting than central state assisted local authority rental housing.

In countries with corporatist systems, by contrast, such housing interests – both profit-seeking landlords and cost rental housing movements – are more likely to be centrally involved in the policy-making process. In some cases they will have a political party to represent their views. And because multi-party political systems are based on compromise and coalition, rental policy strategies that encourage diversity and support different forms of landlordism are much more likely to emerge. The more corporatist and compromise-dependent a political system is, therefore, the more sector interests gain active representation in policy making and the more diverse the rental market is likely to be as a result.

Unitary rental markets can therefore be seen – tentatively at least – as the product of give-and-take and mutual accommodation between the major providers of rental housing in a corporatist political system. The structure of the unitary rental market as a self-balancing market in which some private landlord profit is allowed but tempered by the cost rents charged by non-profit housing landlords provides a general framework for competition that systematically takes account of different interests and their needs. The primary interests that produce such a solution will therefore be private landlords on the one hand and cost rental housing organisations on the other.

How much profit extraction the system allows will vary depending on the relative strengths of the different housing interests. In a system where the labour movement is strong, one might expect cost rental housing to play an active rent-determining role. In countries where the labour movement is weaker, unitary rental markets are more likely to be more heavily dominated by profit landlords.

As we shall see in Part II, there are very substantial differences between societies with unitary rental markets in the manner in which those markets are organised. It might be hypothesised that these differences stem from the different compromise solutions that have emerged in societies with differing constellations of interests, and contrasting balances of power between interest groups.

Another way of putting this might be that corporatist-derived policy strategies may be characterised by greater or lesser degrees of compromise and accommodation, depending on the constellation of interests involved. In countries where one interest group – say private landlords – is more influential, the unitary rental market that develops is likely to give greater scope for private profit. In societies with strong sectional interest based on religion or ethnicity, for example, cost rental housing organisations founded on such sectional interests are likely to play a major part in the manner in which the unitary rental market is structured. Where the labour movement is strong in corporatist societies, the outcome is likely to be a unitary rental market that is dominated – or at least heavily influenced – by public or semi-public cost rental organisations.

The above necessarily sketchy observations of the political institutional and power interest basis of different policy strategies provides no more than a starting point for further discussion and analysis. The above suggestions can be summarised as follows. In the most general terms, whether a country has a unitary rental market or a dualist rental system may be explained in terms of corporatist versus two-party political systems. Dualist systems tend to be found in societies with two-party systems while unitary markets tend to be found in societies with corporatist political structures. Furthermore, variations in the structure of unitary rental markets between countries may perhaps be explained in terms of differences in the organisation of corporatism, in the interests represented and in the balance of power between them.

HIDDEN DIMENSIONS OF POWER: THE CASE OF GENDER

To view rental market structuring in purely interest group representation power terms is to miss other important dimensions of power that tend not be represented by vested interests. One of these is that of gender. Gender inequality comprises one of the major social cleavages in modern society. Yet, as Skocpol (1993) shows, gender issues have been almost totally neglected in welfare and social policy theories. She argues that contrary to these theories, gender is of central importance in determining the nature of social policy regimes in different countries.

The neglect of gender in theories of welfare and social policy is easy to understand. Although gender is clearly an important aspect of welfare, the gender dimension of policy issues rarely constitutes the prime – or even subsidiary – motivation for policy measures. With rare important exceptions, such as child care, the gender debate has been missing from the controversies and political conflicts surrounding the development of welfare states.

The reason for the 'policy-invisibility' of gender in the construction of systems of welfare is the weakness – or often the complete absence – of a politically organised gender lobby. Women in particular have not until very recently begun to organise politically and exert pressure for gender-explicit policy making. Indeed, the importance of labour movements in setting the radical political agenda that has been central in developing modern welfare states may well have undermined gender issues. Trades unions have traditionally been male dominated and it is only in recent decades that rising rates of female wage labour have begun to make a significant impact on this male hegemony. The result has been that the history of the welfare state has been one in which gender issues, while clearly present implicitly in a wide range of decisions, have rarely impacted directly and explicitly on social policy. At best, it has remained what might be termed a 'sotto voce issue' with very low visibility in public debates.

This invisibility of gender issues in the construction of social policy must constitute one of the most dramatic instances of hidden agenda politics in modern history. It has impacted directly on welfare state research, which mirrors the gender inattentiveness of the policy-making process itself.

The all-pervasiveness of gender inequalities, the strong home and family orientation of female roles in modern patriarchal society, and the importance of housing in everyday life mean that housing is one area gender effects impact in a particularly direct manner. After access to wage labour, access to adequate low-cost housing is one of the most important preconditions for gender equality. The ability of women to run their own household independently of a male wage earner is crucially dependent on the availability of housing, and particularly rental housing. With rising rates of divorce and single-parent households, housing that requires no capital investment, that offers security of tenure, and that is based on non-profit rents is a necessary, even if not on its own sufficient, precondition for gender equality.

It is therefore worth considering further the gender implications of different rental market policy strategies. I have argued elsewhere that societies, such as Australia, orientated to high levels of detached house owner occupation tend to also possess societies which have low-density urban areas, high car-ownership rates, low levels of social security provision, and heavily domestic-orientated female roles (Kemeny, 1981a, p. 51; Kemeny, 1983b, Ch. 2). By the same token, Sweden's more collectivised urban form and social security system has been explicitly developed at least in part because of the desire to encourage high rates of full-time career-orientated female labour-market participation (Kemeny, 1992a).

Rental market policy strategies are one dimension of this wider issue. Dualist systems are based on structuring rental markets in such a manner as to maximise the number of households that opt for owner occupation. This is achieved in part by discouraging the emergence of a competitive cost rental sector offering low rents and security of tenure as an alternative to buying.

By structuring housing choice in such a manner that favours owner occupation a built-in bias in favour of two-income households which can afford to buy is created. Single-income households – especially those among lower-income earners – will be severely disadvantaged in gaining access to housing. Given the considerable increase in single-person households, and particularly single-parent households, over the post-war period, and the fact that women are over-represented in these groups, it is clear that dualist systems have highly differential gender implications.

The exclusion of important groups from access to owner occupation in home-owning societies comprises a major source of inequality. Dualist systems provide for no viable alternative to owner occupation for most households. Households with children – and particularly single-parent households – are particularly vulnerable. Unable to afford to buy, they will be forced to 'choose' between private profit renting with its insecurity of tenure and high rents on the one hand and a stigmatised and hard to access public rental sector. It is probably not an exaggeration to say that the choice between a dualist and unitary rental system is the single most important social determinant of the extent of gender inequality for female single-adult households in a society.

Yet despite this it is difficult to pinpoint the political role of the gender issue in the formation of rental policy strategy, except in rare isolated cases, such as Swedish post-war social planning. Gender remains a largely unacknowledged dimension of rental strategic policy making: part of a male-dominated way of thinking.

Penetrating below the surface activity of the policy process that takes place in the circus world of media-orientated politics reveals complex cross currents. The taken-for-granted and apparently obvious explanations of policy making will inevitably be superficial without this. It is here that the hidden agendas and non-decisions of the political process cannot even be perceived – let alone appreciated – without understanding dominant strands of thought left implicit and unspoken.

Part II
Case studies

Introduction

In Part II the discussion moves from conceptual and theoretical considerations to an examination of the different rental strategies and rental
systems that have emerged in a number of countries. The purpose of
this is twofold.

My first concern is to concretise the two types of rental market
strategies through exemplification. In doing this, some of the general
principles underlying the organisation and processes of change found
in both dualist and unitary rental systems that have been presented
and discussed in Part I can be illustrated in the case studies. Public
renting and cost renting have taken different forms in different countries. The maturation process has varied from one country to another.
In addition, historic junctures have taken place at different points in
time, in different political contexts and under different circumstances.
Their outcomes have also varied considerably.

The substantive discussion is in two parts. The first chapter examines and exemplifies the maturation process in one cost rental housing
company in Sweden and one public rental housing agency in Australia.
Drawing on the annual reports and statements of accounts that span
the entire post-war period, this chapter concretises the maturation
process and provides some rough indication of its importance in reducing costs well below profit rent levels. I also examine the impact of
discounted sales on maturation drawing on British data. The following
two chapters take a wider perspective and examine in turn the rental
systems of a number of countries that have pursued command and
market policy strategies.

Second, and equally important in this discussion, is to develop
a more nuanced picture that can form the basis for subsequent conceptual development. This is particularly the case when considering
unitary market strategies. Dualist systems display much less variety,
perhaps because they are based on a policy strategy of the repression

and residualisation of cost renting. While there may be wide differences in the size of the public rental sector, there are not so many different ways in which dualism may be structured. Unitary market strategies are much more diverse and varied. For although unitary rental markets share the same basic broad principles there are considerable differences in the manner in which each policy strategy has developed in different countries. Integrated rental markets can be achieved in any number of different ways. Therefore, market strategies are often highly innovative and ingenious.

Indeed, so great is the variation even among the rather small number of countries with unitary rental markets discussed here that some conceptualisation of the differences is called for. Therefore, in Chapter 9 the broader conceptual issues are returned to. In particular, I try to develop a simple conceptual framework for classifying unitary rental markets and understanding why they differ from one another so greatly.

This framework must be seen as very preliminary. I make no claims that the simple distinction between dualist and unitary strategies is anything more than an initial conceptualisation. It is likely – even highly desirable – that further research will lead to considerable refinement or even the development of alternative frameworks that explain the variations more satisfactorily.

6 Case studies in the maturation process

INTRODUCTION

As noted in Chapter 3, the process of maturation has been almost totally neglected in the public rental housing literature. There are two main reasons for this. In the first place, cost rental and public rental systems are nearly all relatively immature. Their growth is largely limited to the post-war period, which has seen a massive expansion of social renting in many countries. It is really only since the 1970s – and in some countries considerably later – that maturation has accelerated to the extent that it has begun to have a noticeable effect on holding costs down. The reason for this has been a combination of rising inflation and falling rates of new production. This acceleration in maturation has varied from country to country both in its rate and in its timing.

But the neglect of the maturation process is also due to the manner in which policy debates have been conducted: with no reference at all to maturation and by diverting attention from the impact of maturation on rent levels to the role of state subsidies. This has led to the widely held belief that social rents are low because of public subsidies, and has served to divert attention from the impact of the maturation process on the determination of rent levels.

In this chapter I attempt to quantify the impact of maturation on the debt structure of cost rental housing by looking in some detail at two examples. My purpose here is to present supporting evidence for the assertion made in this study that maturation reduces costs significantly; even dramatically. One argument that has been made at seminars and in general discussions of earlier versions of this study has been that maturation is not in fact as important as I have made out, and that the differences in costs between cost renting and profit renting are not so great as to constitute the basis for policy strategy.

The only way this kind of argument can be met is to produce time series data to demonstrate the dimensions of the impact of maturation. I do so by presenting case studies of cost rental housing during the post-war period.

The process of maturation can be illustrated in a somewhat abstract manner with the help of the following hypothetical computer-generated simulation (Table 2). This assumes that a cost rental company builds one new standard dwelling a year, starting in year 1, that it does so with a 100 per cent loan amortised over 25 years at a fixed rate of interest of 10 per cent a year, and that each year the cost of building a new standard dwelling rises by 5 per cent. Running costs per dwelling for the whole stock – administration, maintenance, repairs, insurance, taxes etc. – are assumed to be 2 per cent of the construction cost of a new dwelling.

Table 2 Hypothetical model of the maturation process

Year	Construction price	Total costs (running costs and debt-charges/amortisation) of a new dwelling	Pooled cost-rent
01	1,000.00	130.17	130.17
05	1,215.51	158.22	146.06
10	1,551.33	201.93	169.59
15	1,979.93	257.72	198.08
20	2,526.95	328.93	232.68
25	3,225.10	419.81	274.82
30	4,116.14	533.79	306.01
35	5,253.35	683.82	349.77
40	6,704.75	872.74	407.37
45	8,557.15	1,113.87	481.17
50	10,921.33	1,203.18	574.54
55	13,938.70	1,814.37	691.95
60	17,789.70	2,315.65	839.18

Source: Adapted from Kemeny (1981a), Table 2.1, p. 23.

The pooled cost rent is the rent needed to cover the costs of the total stock and it is found by adding on the running costs of the year in question to the sum of the interest and amortisation on all the dwellings. It can be seen that the cost rent rises more slowly than the total cost of new dwellings, so that by year 60 the cost rent is only 36 per cent of the total cost of a new dwelling. The growing gap between these is accounted for almost entirely by the fact that the size of new loans calls forth a much higher debt-servicing charge than the average of the outstanding loans. A secondary factor is the amortisation of existing loans.

In real life, maturation is affected by a wide range of factors. Falling rates of newbuild – such as in this hypothetical example, where the addition of one new dwelling a year represents a falling rate of newbuild – accelerate the maturation process while a stable inflation rate of only 5 per cent will decelerate the process of maturation. The above abstract model is therefore only useful as a rough indication of the expected impact of maturation.

CHOICE OF CASE STUDIES

The following case studies have been chosen from two countries – Sweden and Australia – with radically different rental policy strategies, complemented by a very preliminary investigation of the impact of discounted sales on maturation in Australia and Britain. The national rental housing policies of the countries concerned is dealt with in the next chapter and will not be discussed here. The concern in this chapter is rather to illustrate how the process of maturation is common to both dualist and unitary rental systems and so constitutes the shared economic basis upon which different policy strategies can then be built. One cost rental company can never be 'representative' of a country's total stock of cost rental housing, but in choosing a case study my intention is to illustrate through a concrete example the broad trends in the process of maturation in general that cost rental housing has reached in the country concerned.

The Swedish and Australian case studies are chosen from cost rental housing organisations that have built up a rental stock over an extended period without being disrupted by large-scale discounted sales, which distort the maturation process. The discussion of the impact of discounted sales on the maturation process later in the chapter draws on data from more than one agency.

METHODOLOGICAL PROBLEMS IN USING ANNUAL REPORTS

In the case studies I use the organisations' annual reports and the accompanying financial statements produced for the annual audit. This is normally publicly available and provides a detailed overview of the organisation's operations, usually stretching back in an unbroken series to the inception of the organisation.

Comparable information is not normally available for private profit rental housing since much of this is provided by individuals rather than by companies. Even when the housing is provided by a private company it will often be just one of a number of operations that the company runs and so will not be clearly separated out as an independent item for scrutiny.

Public and cost rental housing companies, by contrast, are often – though, as we shall see, by no means always – obliged to produce accessible annual reports and to make their annual financial statements available. The quality of, and accessibility of, such reports does vary considerably, however. Australian public housing agencies produce much more detailed and useful annual reports than British councils do for their housing operations.

Annual reports are an astonishingly neglected source of data on public and cost rental housing.[1] Yet they are invaluable for studying the process of maturation in cost rental housing, and, indeed, for many other aspects of the operations of public and cost rental housing. The financial statements are a particularly useful source for the analysis of trends in costs, rents, rent rebates, and other economic indices of performance. In addition, the annual reports often contain much useful serial data on social aspects of operations, including waiting lists, the social groups that are in receipt of rent rebates, and sometimes more general data on the local housing market. The regular production of annual reports also means that they can be used to build up a picture of the operations of the organisations over extended periods.

The two individual case studies focus on slightly different aspects of the maturation problematic. This is partly because the data is presented in slightly different ways in the two sets of annual reports. Thus, for example, it is possible to trace the investment history and changing debt structure of individual properties in the Swedish accounts. This sheds light on the process of maturation as it is affected by the investment histories of individual properties. In the Australian accounts this is not possible. To take another example, the Australian accounts allow a more direct comparison between debt structures and newbuild construction costs than the Swedish accounts. This means that this crucial variable has to be analysed in a more indirect manner in the Swedish case.

In addition to differences that derive from the way in which the annual accounts are organised, the different rental systems that these housing organisations are part of also impact on how they may be analysed. Public rental or cost rental housing relates to profit rental housing and to the wider social security system in different ways in dualist and unitary rental markets.

Thus, for example, in the Swedish case it is not very fruitful to compare the rents charged by the cost rental housing organisation with those charged by private profit-orientated rental organisations, since private rents are largely determined by the cost structure of cost rental organisations (see the section on Sweden in Chapter 8). In Australia such comparisons are both possible and useful because public housing rents are not permitted to impact directly on profit rents. For this reason, the Australian case study includes a section on rents that is omitted from the Swedish case study.

Much the same goes for the study of rent rebates. In Sweden these are paid out of the national and local public budgets and so do not affect the operations of cost rental organisations. In Australia they are paid out of the rent surpluses charged by public rental housing agencies, and so impact directly on rents.

It is worth bearing in mind that the financial statements of companies pose special problems for the purposes for which they have been used here. Such statements are not primarily intended for research purposes. They are produced to provide a justification for the existence of the company and as evidence that its economic affairs are being well taken care of. They also mirror the power relationship between the state and the organisation producing the statements and are often structured to produce information that conforms with political expectations. They therefore constitute a special kind of gloss of reality. Because of this, they must be used with caution, and findings based on them must be taken as only very general and broad indications of wider social and economic processes that researchers are often interested in.

There are additional problems in using statements that cover several years in order to draw out longer-term trends. In the first place, the organisation of company reports and statements often undergoes considerable changes from time to time, in which the categories used in one period often do not correspond at all to those used at another time. More treacherously, the categories used at different times may appear to be the same but may in fact not be.

Because of such pitfalls my analysis of the maturation process is carried out at a very general level. I have had to use the most general categories of data that I felt gave sufficient indication of the phenomena I was interested in but which must therefore only be taken as crude indices rather than accurate and detailed measures. Where special problems of this sort have arisen I have indicated this.

SWEDEN: GAVLEGÅRDARNA

The cost rental housing company of Gavlegårdarna in the town of Gåvle is the oldest in Sweden. Its first dwellings were brought into service in 1917 and it has been building cost rental housing ever since. Like all Swedish cost rental housing it is organised in the form of a company with a majority shareholding belonging to the local government in which it operates. The organisation of Swedish cost renting can therefore be likened to what is becoming known in Britain as 'arms-length' housing. Gävle is a medium-sized town by Swedish standards and is fairly average by most major statistical indices for the country as a whole, including its housing.

Before looking at the data it is useful to clarify some of the problems that have arisen in their interpretation. In the first place, although a distinction is made in the reports throughout the post-war period between mortgages on existing properties (*inteckningslån*) and building credit on properties in the process of being built (*byggnadskreditiv*), in some years the distinction could not be sustained because some dwellings were completed during the process of construction (i.e. while the building credit was still being used but before the property was mortgaged).

Furthermore, it was not always clear from the reports that this was so. This meant that it was not possible for me to accurately detail the amount of front loading that was taking place each year. I therefore resorted to lumping both sorts of loan together and comparing one year with the next. This meant that in years when there was a large amount of newbuild taking place, heavy front-end loading disproportionately inflated the total outstanding debt. I have chosen to accept this simplification and regard the data as merely generally indicative of longer-term trends.

Another problem concerned the occasional sale of existing properties, as took place, for example, in 1957. Rather than specify the sum received for the sale the accounting procedure deducted the proceeds from outstanding loans and it was not possible to determine the price obtained from this as this one-off amortisation was subsumed under the total value of all amortisations.

It might also be noted that outstanding debt includes debt on other facilities such as shopping centres, day-care centres, and the growing involvement of the company in other activities such as the provision of owner occupied housing and also of infrastructure. This is clearly evidenced in the falling share of housing rents as a proportion of total income from 97 per cent of total expenditure in both 1945 and 1967 to

86 per cent in 1978, after which changes in the accounting system used make direct comparisons impossible. Nevertheless, housing has always constituted by far the most important activity of the company. In so far as other investment has increased in recent years any inaccuracies this may create will operate to down-value the impact of the maturation process, and thereby contribute to drawing conservative conclusions.

Finally, I make a more general observation. The annual reports become less detailed and less informative as time passes, while they also become more attractive presentationally. From 1917 to 1960 each property was listed and full details were provided on the acquisition value (*anskaffningsvärde*) and rental income of each property, as well as other information such as depreciation, taxation value and fire insurance value. In 1962 the rental income of some properties began to be combined, and this became more common as the company's property portfolio grew. In 1966 the category of 'rental income' was broadened to 'income' (*intäkter*). In 1973 the category of income was removed entirely. In 1979 the entire list over properties detailing their acquisition values, depreciation, unamortised loan amounts and taxation value (a table which in 1978 had run into seven pages) was henceforth omitted. The year 1979 also saw the introduction of a new A4 report with a coloured cover. In 1982 the reports began to appear on glossy paper, with colour photography and taking up more general and popular concerns such as tenant influence, decentralisation and cable television. The general trend, over a considerable span of time, has therefore been away from detailed data presentation and towards attractive presentation, readability and generalities.

The maturation process

Data was collected for every year from 1945 to 1990 inclusive, on the total outstanding debt and the number of dwellings. The total outstanding debt was then divided by the number of dwellings to obtain average outstanding debt per dwelling per year. This is summarised in Table 3.

To obtain a general indication of the growing gap between outstanding debt and new debt, I divided the increase in total debt in a given year by the increase in the number of dwellings in that year. In some years the result was bizarre, probably as a result of heavy borrowing for infrastructure development that year. However, the general trend is clear, with the gap between average outstanding debt and average new debt growing to quite dramatic proportions by 1990 (see Table 4).

Table 3 Gavlegårdarna's stock and average outstanding debt,
1945–90

Year	No. of dwellings	Average debt per dwelling
1945	345	12,327
1950	929	17,417
1955	1,645	25,312
1960	2,534	32,618
1965	3,475	39,175
1970	6,059	44,073
1975	8,160	56,880
1980	8,648	71,158
1985	9,667	101,696
1990	9,975	141,692

Source: Gavlegårdarna, *Annual Reports and Accounts*, Gävle, 1945–90.

Table 4 Gavlegårdarna's average outstanding debt and average newbuild
debt, per dwelling, SEK, selected years

Year	Dwgs built no.	Average debt per dwg SEK	Average debt per new dwg SEK	Ratio of new to total debt
1947	206	13,367	13,693	1.02:1
1959	211	32,875	34,062	1.04:1
1964	225	37,543	65,234	1.74:1
1967	565	44,561	57,954	1.30:1
1969	622	48,902	56,302	1.21:1
1973	560	56,720	58,430	1.03:1
1974	188	57,854	112,626	1.95:1
1976	082	57,943	163,779	2.83:1
1980	262	71,158	251,614	3.54:1
1985	184	101,696	414,291	4.07:1
1987	094	120,974	714,809	5.91:1
1988	012	122,986	975,417	7.93:1
1990	126	141,692	1,490,159	10.52:1

Source: Gavlegårdarna, *Annual Reports and Accounts*, Gävle, 1947–90, selected years.

The figures for average debt per new dwelling are roughly comparable to figures published for the whole of Sweden in the *Yearbook of
Housing and Building Statistics*. This is a useful check on the validity
of the accounts data, especially bearing in mind the approximate
nature of the debt data in Gavlegårdarna's accounts as discussed
earlier. The national data begin in 1965 when the average production

cost of a flat was 70,300 kr, somewhat more that the average debt on a new Gavlegårdarna dwelling (the great majority of which are flats). This is roughly in line with production cost differences between the town of Gåvle and the whole of Sweden. In 1974 the average national production cost of a flat rose to 101,700 kr, in 1985 to 460,700 kr. After this the gap grows dramatically, the reasons for which I will return to.

It can be seen that the gap between outstanding and new debt remains very modest until 1964. Maturation took place only very slowly until the 1960s, indicating the very long-term nature of the maturation process and its almost imperceptible course. It needs to be born in mind that although the Million Programme[2] decade of 1965 to 1974 (during which one million dwellings were built) were ones of spectacular absolute numbers of new dwellings, the late 1940s and 1950s were years of far more rapid stock expansion in terms of per-centage increases in stock. Thus, in 1947 the increase in stock was no less than 50 per cent (206 dwellings added to a stock in 1946 of 414 dwellings). In 1949 it was 26 per cent, and in 1953 it was 20 per cent.

The rate of growth fell gradually, throughout the period, being lower in some years than in others but in 1957 – a year when produc-tion rose to 294 dwellings – the rate of accretion was still 29 per cent. In comparison, the Million Programme years showed puny rates of increase. Thus, in 1967 when 565 new dwellings were built this only represented a 16 per cent increase. In 1969 when 622 dwellings were built – an all-time record – the rate of increase fell to 14 per cent. Then in 1973 when 560 new dwellings were built this only represented an 8 per cent increase. The only year the rate of increase matched those of the 1940s was 1970 when, as a result of a takeover of another cost rental housing company (Valbohem) and its 800 dwellings, on the integration of Valbo kommun with Gävle kommun the stock increased by 20 per cent.[3]

Despite the lower relative rate of stock accretion during the Million Programme, front loading was sufficiently heavy to reduce the ratio of old to new debt per dwelling – the maturation index – to near parity. Between 1964 and 1973 the maturation index fell from 1.74 to 1.03, back to early 1950s levels. Equally striking is the rapid maturation that took place during the 1970s and particularly after the Million Programme when the high vacancy rate led to drastically reduced newbuild. But most impressive of all is the dramatic acceleration in maturation that took place during the late 1980s, a time of rapid construction cost inflation combined with low rates of newbuild.

However, the late 1980s were also a time when there was a decline in newbuild in favour of modernisation, and here a word of caution is required when interpreting the dramatic increase in the maturation index in more recent years. The debt per new dwelling is inflated in all years by the use of some loan money for renovation and modernisation. An accurate picture of the average debt per new dwelling would therefore take this into account, by separating out investment in modernisation from that in newbuild. This is not possible in the accounts where the costs of modernising old dwellings are not separately accounted from the debt per new dwelling.

This accounts for at least some of the extra cost of producing a new dwelling over national production figures, but most particularly during the late 1980s when hardly any new dwellings were built but considerable investment in modernisation took place. Thus, for example, in 1988 national production costs per flat were 700,300 kr compared to a per new dwelling Gavlegårdarna debt of 975,417 ascribed to a new production of only 12 newly acquired dwellings but in fact including much modernisation work on existing stock.

It is therefore important to treat the dramatic increase in the maturation index as shown in Table 4 with considerable caution. The 1988 ratio, for example, is also almost certainly considerably less than 10:1. If we assume that the amount of debt allocated to building the 12 new dwellings in 1988 corresponds to national production costs in that year of 700,300 kr per dwelling rather than the actual debt of 975,417 per dwelling, this gives a ratio of new to old debt on newly built Gavlegårdarna dwellings in 1988 of less than 6:1.

Even then, it needs to be remembered that a portion of the higher debt on newer dwellings is accounted for by higher standards. In particular there has been an increase in the number of rooms and floor areas of flats over the years, while more and better facilities are generally provided (such as freezers, dishwashers, better insulation, lifts). But even if we accept this much lower ratio as more accurate and depress it still further by a generous amount to account for higher housing standards – say by almost half to 3:1 – it still represents a dramatic increase in maturation since the Million Programme. A maturation index of 3 is quite impressive in terms of its impact on rent levels.

The changing debt structure of one property: Skyttegården

The process of maturation may be illustrated by looking at the way in which one property changes its relationship to the stock as a whole in terms of relative debt-burden. The property in the block known as

Skyttegården on Valbogatan near what is now the centre of Gävle was built during 1945 and in occupation by 1946. It comprised 69 flats of which 23 had one room plus kitchen and bathroom and 46 had 2 rooms plus kitchen and bathroom. The property cost SEK1,264,122 to build, or SEK18,321 per flat, compared to an average per dwelling debt for the whole stock then of SEK13,205. The ratio of the outstanding debt on the property to the total outstanding per dwelling debt in that year was therefore 1.39:1.

By 1978 – the last year in which individual property details are provided – the average debt per dwelling had risen to SEK60,294 while the debt per dwelling for a property roughly comparable to Skyttegården, built in 1977 and taken into occupancy in 1978 can be seen from the case of the property given the description, Forsbacka 3:34 and 3:35, comprising 58 flats. This had 16 flats of 1 room, kitchen and bathroom, 16 of 2 rooms, kitchen and bathroom, 20 of 3 rooms, kitchen and bathroom and 6 of 4 rooms kitchen and bathroom. The property cost SEK8,669,883 to build, or an average per flat of SEK149,481. This property therefore had a ratio of debt to existing debt per dwelling of 2.48:1, and cost over eight times more per flat to build than Skyttegården.

Skyttegården was fully modernised in 1989 and after converting previously commercial space into housing comprised 71 flats (an increase of 2 flats). This completes the first cycle of that particular property through its contribution to the maturation process. In 1989 Skyttegården must be considered to be to all intents and purposes a new property in so far as its contribution to the maturation process is concerned, and as time passes the ratio of its new debt (not shown in the accounts) to the average debt per dwelling will again begin to fall.

Gavlegårdarna as an index of maturation nationally

There is no reason to believe that Gavlegårdarna's housing stock is exceptionally mature in comparison with other cost rental housing companies. The early origins of the company only gave a very marginal advantage to Gavlegårdarna since although the rate of accretion was very high, the actual numbers of new housing built was extremely modest before 1945. Between 1917 and 1945 only 345 dwellings were acquired, representing an average newbuild over the whole period of less than 13 dwellings a year. Those 345 dwellings – many of which have since either been sold or modernised – only comprise 3.5 per cent of Gavlegårdarna's total stock of 9,975 dwellings in 1990.

The growing maturation of Gavlegårdarna's housing stock therefore suggests that much the same process, at least in its broadest outlines has been taking place in the Swedish cost rental housing stock as a whole. The process of maturation of Gavlegårdarna's stock has been very slow until the mid-1970s. Since then maturation has accelerated, providing the economic circumstances for new directions in rental housing policy.

In Chapter 3 I suggest that major systemic changes in rental systems tend to take place at historic junctures when the maturation process has been accelerating rapidly. The evidence from Gavlegårdarna is that a rapid process of maturation has been taking place since the mid-1970s. Maturation has accelerated even further in the late 1980s, and, because of the current low rates of newbuild and declines in major renovation investment programmes, this acceleration is likely to continue well into the 1990s. Indeed, decisions to withdraw subsidy can be expected to lead to yet still further reductions in demand for new housing and so sustain the acceleration of maturation.

AUSTRALIA: THE SOUTH AUSTRALIAN HOUSING TRUST

The South Australian Housing Trust is, like Gavlegårdarna, the oldest extant cost rental housing organisation in the country, having commenced operations in 1936, two decades later than its Swedish counterpart. It differs from Gavlegårdarna in that its stock is predominantly made up of detached and semi-detached houses rather than flats.

The trust has the largest share of dwellings of any Australian state housing agency, accounting for around 10 per cent of dwellings in South Australia. Unlike most other state housing agencies it has not engaged in large-scale discounted sales of its rental stock to sitting tenants, although it does sell some houses and also has a separate build-for-sale programme. Nor did the trust ever become involved in the high-rise boom that took place in New South Wales and most particularly in neighbouring Victoria, and it is only in recent years that some acquisition of strata title low rise flats has taken place.

An important reason for this difference is that the South Australian state government used public renting as a means of encouraging immigration and industrial development, especially during the 1940s and 1950s. It did this by providing cost rent housing in order to aid in the recruitment of migrant workers and lower the cost of labour, thereby encouraging investment in industrial development. Thus, for example, in Whyalla, the state's second largest city originally based on major shipbuilding and steel works, over 70 per cent of housing was public rental.

Of all the state housing agencies, then, the trust has operated most like a cost rental housing organisation and with a considerable degree of autonomy, a status that is reflected in its being called a trust rather than a Commission, as is the case in the other states. As a result its stock of housing has attained a considerably higher level of maturation than in the other states. By the mid-1970s, for example, average outstanding debt per dwelling was under $10,000 compared to between $12,000 and $25,000 in the other five states.

Data sources: the annual reports

The trust produces annual reports and financial statements. In contrast to Gavlegårdarna, whose annual reports have become less informative in recent years, the trust annual reports have become more detailed and more informative. In particular, a special supplement has been produced each year since 1982, called *Housing in Focus* which provides a wealth of statistical detail on the South Australian housing market, the trust waiting list, and a range of social dimensions of trust operations, including rent rebate schemes, emergency housing, joint ventures and renovation programmes.

This is not to deny that there are problems in using this data source. Some of these are similar to those described in the previous section on Gavlegårdarna. This can be illustrated with the example of construction costs. As in all financial statements, capital investments in any year will include expenditure on both dwellings started and completed, and so it will not be immediately clear exactly how much each dwelling cost to build, nor exactly how much of each dwelling was financed with federal and state government low-interest loans, own capital and private loans.

However, it is normally possible to deduce this from examination of other parts of the statement, and where this is not possible the accuracy of the amounts can be cross checked against other data, for example on average house price construction statistics in the state. In more recent years the supplements often provide additional information that either gives the actual figures needed or facilitates a more accurate estimate.

The maturation process

The growth of the trust's housing stock follows the usual pattern of very rapid expansion from a small initial stock, with annual percentage increases in the stock staying normally well above 20 per cent until the early 1950s. The decline in front loading becomes marked during the second half of the 1950s though the percentage increase in the housing stock stayed in double figures until 1959. Even after this the annual increases in the stock remained between 8 and 9 per cent until 1963 when it fell to 6 per cent, then 4 years later to 5 per cent. For the next ten years the rate of increase remained at between 2 and 3 per cent a year, rising from 1978 to first 4 then 5 per cent where it stayed until 1987. In the following 3 years it fell still further to between 3 and 1 per cent, though it is too early to know whether this low level will be sustained through the 1990s.

Front loading is only one factor affecting maturation. Equally important are other factors such as inflation in construction costs. Table 5 shows the way in which maturation has increased over the last half century.

Table 5 Debt structure of trust rental stock, 1938–88

Year	Rental stock (a)	Outstanding public debt (b)	Mean debt per dwelling (c)	Mean construction cost per dwelling (d)	Debt as % of construction (c as % of d)
1938	84	£36,456	£434	£434	100
1948	3,311	£2,905,519	£702	£878	80
1958	19,687	£44,267,746	£2,249	£4,000	56
1968	30,108	$175,658,030	$5,834	$11,000	53
1978	40,129	$380,578,460	$9,484	$29,000	33
1988	60,655	$945,273,000	$15,584	$47,998	32

Source: Trust Annual Reports.

The biggest increases in maturation have taken place during the 1950s and the 1970s. The 1950s were marked by rapidly falling front loading as the rate of stock accretion fell towards single figures. The 1970s were a period of very modest front loading, with increases in the stock of between 2 and 3 per cent a year. This was the slowest rate of increase of any decade either before or after the 1970s. By contrast, the 1980s were a decade of considerable increase in front loading, when the rate of new additions rose to 5 per cent – a virtual doubling of the rate compared to the preceding decade. As a result, very little maturation took place during the 1980s.

The 1970s were therefore a period of rapid maturation. The impact of this was, as we shall see in the next chapter, accentuated by rapidly rising private rents and a growing gap between public and private rents. It was this growing gap that was at least one reason for the introduction by the federal government of market rents in public renting in 1978. It is therefore instructive to examine the trust's rent structure to see how this changed and impacted on the annual balance sheet.

Rents and rent rebates

Prior to 1979 rent setting in trust housing operated on the basis of a variant of individual historic cost rents. That is, rents directly reflected the cost structure of individual dwellings, or more specifically the cost structure of particular dwelling types and sizes on individual estates for as long as a household remained in the dwelling. This meant that the real value of rents fell as the dwelling aged and as long as it was still occupied by the same household. Once the dwelling was vacated the rent of the relet dwelling was adjusted upwards to comply with approximately average current economic rent values, which was roughly comparable to the cost rent on a new dwelling. This rent was termed the 'vacancy rent'.

One consequence of this system of rent setting is that annual rental income was strongly affected by the vacancy rate of the stock, over and above the rate of newbuild. In general, in years when more vacancies were created rental income rose faster than in years when fewer vacancies occurred. This picture is further complicated by the fact that tenants who moved from one trust dwelling to another but who were in receipt of rent rebates may or may not have freed up their vacated dwelling to a household not in receipt of rebates, while, because they themselves were eligible for rent rebates, they would not pay the vacancy rent in the dwelling to which they moved. Their 'rebate' would also rise to reflect the higher nominal rent of the new dwelling.

This rent-setting system impacted on net rental receipts in a variable and unpredictable manner. Thus, for example, rental income increased in 1976 by 30 per cent, in 1977 by 24 per cent and in 1978 by 18 per cent. However, in 1979 rent receipts fell by 2 per cent.

Since 1979 the policy has been to move away from individual historic cost based rents and gradually adjust all rents upward to vacancy rent levels. This is in accord with the market rent policy introduced in the 1978 Commonwealth-State Housing Agreement. This transition to vacancy rents, or what, under the new regime, might be more accurately termed 'construction cost rents' (since it is based on the rent that would cover the cost of providing a new dwelling) involves moving away completely from the concept of cost rental housing as I use the term here and towards a rent-setting system which generates overall surpluses. In fact, surpluses are not made, because these are used to rebate the rents of low-income tenants.

This notional surplus is therefore used to pay low-income tenants rent rebates which, had the recipients been private tenants, would have been paid out of publicly funded social security. In effect, then, public tenants are subsidising the taxpayer to the extent that they provide the rent rebates out of the difference between historic costs and newbuild construction costs. Indeed, the savings are greater, because a proportion of rebates to private tenants goes towards sustaining the profits of private landlords. It is therefore necessary to look a little closer at rent rebating in order to understand the extent to which rents reflect costs.

The increases in rents that the move to market rents has involved have resulted in a dramatic increase in the number of trust tenants in receipt of rent rebates. This rose from 9 per cent of tenants in 1974 to 51 per cent in 1981. The number of tenants in receipt of rent rebates has steadily risen since then to reach 69 per cent in 1990 and 71 per cent in 1991.

A proportion of this increase is due to existing tenants who previously had paid full historic cost rents finding that their rents have risen to the point at which, due to the high proportion of their income which is spent on rents, they become eligible for rent rebates. The rest of the increase will come from a combination of better-off tenants leaving the trust to find alternative housing – often by buying into owner occupation – and fewer medium-income earners applying for trust housing for the same reason.

The impact of this on trust rents has been considerable. In effect, the trust makes considerable surpluses on its rental operations. Since rent rebating is provided on a graded scale, depending on income, and since 70 per cent of tenants receive some sort of rent rebate, rebates come only partly from the rents of unrebated tenants. An unknown proportion must also come from the rents of tenants on less than full rebates. Indeed, in theory it is possible that tenants on full rebates may in some cases be paying rents net of rebates that are higher than would be the case if they were charged rents that reflected strict historic costs. Table 6 shows how the move to market rents has impacted on the scale of rent rebate cross subsidisation.

To appreciate the impact of rent rebating it is necessary to compare the average annual rent rebate of $1,491 in 1990 (1991 Annual Report)

Table 6 Trust rent rebates, 1975–90, selected years

Year	Rent before rebates ($m)	Rent rebates	
		Total ($m)	Per tenant ($)
1975	28.1	1.4	4
1980	58.2	7.5	175
1985	127.1	36.6	687
1990	168.8	92.4	1,491

Source: Trust Annual Reports.

with average unrebated rents. The average annual rent for a standard five-room semi-detached trust house in Metropolitan Adelaide in 1990 was $4,000, and for a standard five-room detached trust house was $5,720. From this it may be deduced that trust market rents in 1990 were very roughly between 25 and 40 per cent higher than cost rents.

How do these rent levels compare with private profit rents? The 1991 Annual Report cites figures obtained from the residential tenancies tribunal of average private rents for houses of $147 a week, or $7,700 a year. This puts trust rents at approximately 75 per cent of the level of private rental market rents. In 1982, the first year for which the annual reports provide statistics on this, trust rents were 54 per cent of private rents.

In the last decade, then, rent differentials between private and trust rents have narrowed considerably. Much of this decrease must be put down to the move to increase rent levels to construction cost rents in the trust stock. Since trust rents are some 75 per cent of private profit rents and trust rents themselves are up to 40 per cent higher than strict cost covering rents, we may conclude that had the trust been operating as a true cost rental housing trust, cost covering rents would be some 30 to 40 per cent those of private rents.

This compares quite well with the debt-to-construction-cost ratio of 32 per cent given in Table 5. In other words, since average debt per trust dwelling is only 32 per cent of average debt per new trust dwelling, giving us a ratio of averaging existing debt to average new debt of 1:3 or a maturation index of 3, we would expect to find that the ratio between trust rents – were these based on cost rents – and private rents was also 1:3.

Compared to the cost–profit rent ratio of 1:3, the actual ratio of trust to private rents of 1:1.25 is dramatically higher. This indicates the success of the market rent strategy. Of course, the surpluses produced by the trust in this context are largely notional, as they are given back to tenants in the form of rent rebates. What is the point of this account juggling and the consequent rent-to-rebate money carousel? It only serves to stigmatise the recipients of rent rebates. These would otherwise take the form of imputed rental income accruing to the tenants of a cost rental housing organisation.

The only conceivable point of the exercise can be to deter the better off tenants from applying for trust housing or to 'encourage' (in the sense of using the stick rather than the carrot) the better-off to leave. Here we see how the federal government command policy towards public renting impacts directly on the lives of ordinary households both by channelling their choice of housing and by stigmatising whole groups of households as rent rebate recipients.

MATURATION AND ASSET STRIPPING: DISCOUNTED SALES

Do discounted sales increase cost rents?

The impact of the sale of cost rental housing on rents has been almost totally neglected in the housing literature. The reason for this seems to be a widespread belief that it makes little difference to rents if a dwelling is sold. As long as the receipts from the sale allow the outstanding debt to be paid off, the rents of the remaining tenants will not be adversely affected. This is, at best, a dubious assumption to make.

To illustrate this, consider the following hypothetical example from Table 2 above. Let us assume that in year 60 the cost rental organisation sells its oldest dwelling to the current tenant. Due to depreciation, the valuation will normally be somewhat below the price of a new dwelling built in year 60. If the valuation system estimates the value of the dwelling from the return received on the cost rent of the dwelling, this would yield a valuation roughly equivalent to a dwelling build in year 50.

Let us further assume that a 60 per cent discount on valuation – quite a common size of discount in command systems of public renting – is granted to the tenant. This means the year 1 dwelling is sold for approximately £6,550 (60 per cent of the cost of a dwelling built in year 50). Since there is no outstanding debt on the sold dwelling this amount can then be set off against the 100 per cent mortgage used to build the year 60 dwelling. A year 60 dwelling can therefore be built with a reduced size mortgage, equivalent to that needed to build a year 50 dwelling.

In effect, a year 1 dwelling is being replaced by a year 60 dwelling built at the cost of a year 50 dwelling. This clearly retards the maturation process that would have taken place had the sale not been made. In our model, the cost of the year 1 dwelling (amounting to the running costs only, in year 60) of £355.79 is being replaced by the same running costs for a year 60 dwelling plus the debt-servicing charges and amortisation of a year 50 dwelling (£1,203.18) instead of debt-servicing and amortisation of a year 60 dwelling. The impact of this on the structure of the stock will be that in year 60 no net increase in stock will take place, the number of dwellings remaining at 59.

The impact of this set of transactions on rents will be as follows. Rent pooling yields an average rent of £839.18 in year 60 assuming no sale. The sale of the year 1 dwelling and its replacement by the costs of a year 50 dwelling means that the cost of the new dwelling with a year 50 dwelling mortgage (plus running costs), totalling £1,340.54 is added to the pooled rent while the cost of the sold year 1 dwelling – running costs of £355.79 – is deducted from the pooled rent. It can be readily seen that this amounts to an additional debt-burden of nearly £1,000, which divided by the total stock of 59 dwellings yields an average pooled rent per dwelling that is £16.70 more than would have been the case had the sale not been made.

This example illustrates the de-maturation impact of discounted sales. The rents of the remaining tenants are increased. In effect, the remaining tenants are subsidising the purchasing tenant, and the greater the discount on valuation price the greater the subsidy. We might note here that, in this hypothetical situation, even if no discount is granted, a slight de-maturation process will have taken place reflecting the difference between the sale price and the cost of replacement that is caused by depreciation. This need not always be the case, however. It is conceivable that the price matches or even exceeds replacement costs, for example, if the location value of the dwelling is particularly high. However, since heavy discounting is the norm in the sale of public rental dwellings it is not unreasonable to conclude that this almost always negatively affects the maturation process of the stock.

Of course, in a real situation rather than a hypothetical simulation it is difficult to measure the impact of discounted sales on rents because so many different factors change at the same time. The best that can be achieved without conducting a major research project on this question is to find circumstantial empirical evidence of the impact of discounted sales on the cost structure of rental housing.

Empirical evidence

The impact of discounted sales on the maturation of public rental housing needs to be determined through a careful analysis of the annual reports of a public rental agency that has conducted a sales programme. Neither of the two organisations examined above have had such a programme. The trust is an outstanding exception to the Australian rule in this sense. Sales have been a major part of most state housing policies for much of the post-war period. Indeed, it is largely because the trust had not sold rental dwellings that it now has the largest stock of any state housing agency – 10 per cent as against a national average of half this.

In Kemeny (1981c) I presented some of the evidence of the impact of discounted sales in a comparison of the trust and the Victoria Housing Commission. This suggested clearly that the sales policy of the Commission had increased the costs of the remaining stock substantially. The impact of this on debt-loads can be crudely demonstrated in that by the late 1970s the average per dwelling outstanding government debt on the trust stock was only 58 per cent that of the Victoria Housing Commission (Kemeny, 1980, Table 2, p. 111).

This evidence can be supplemented by that I have been able to glean on the impact of the so-called 'right to buy' in British council housing. In sharp contrast to both Sweden and Australia, British councils have not published annual reports of their housing operations. This reflects the fact that council housing has been inextricably part of the wider obligations of councils. Statements of housing revenue and capital accounts are in theory available. In practice, because of local government reorganisations and boundary changes and because of variable archiving, finding a council with complete historical records is not easy.[4] Even when this obstacle is overcome, frequent category changes in the accounts to fit the temporary exigencies of local government finance often make it difficult, if not impossible, to carry out useful time series analyses.

The absence of systematic and published annual reports on the oldest and one of the largest stocks of public rental housing in the world is lamentable and a reflection of the lack of public accountability of council housing. Other sources do exist, however. As a second best, I have gleaned information on the impact of council house sales on the maturation process from the records of the Chartered Institute of Public Finance and Accountancy (CIPFA) which are assembled from returns made by councils. These second-hand summaries of highly digested and multiply processed statistics are a standard source of data in housing research. However, they are to be treated with extreme caution as a source of reliable information. In addition, categories change from time to time, making time series analysis difficult.

I present here two aspects of maturation that can be gleaned from CIPFA data: age structure as an index of maturation; and outstanding debt. Table 7 illustrates the general impact of council house sales between 1977 and 1983. This period covers the first two years only of large-scale sales. Yet the impact on the age structure of the stock is quite marked.

It can be seen that in purely age terms the stocks of these councils have become younger. it goes without saying that we may rule out the possibility that this has been caused by a dramatic increase in new-build during the period. The only possible explanation is the impact of council house sales. It is almost certain that this trend has become even more marked throughout the 1980s. In some councils where sales were very high, the decline in the proportion of pre-1945 dwellings was considerably higher. In Enfield, Greater London, for example, the pre-1945 stock fell 10 per cent in a mere three years – from 33 per cent in 1980 to 23 per cent in 1983.

But if the stock has become younger in its age profile, what has happened to its debt-profile? Table 8 shows this for the Greater London Council (and, since its abolition, the councils of which it was comprised).

It can be seen that the stock of Greater London Council (and after its abolition the summed stocks of its borough councils) was more

Table 7 Age distribution of dwellings of selected councils' housing stock, 1977–83 (%)

Council	Year	Pre-1945	1945–64	Post-1964	Total
Manchester	1977	33	31	36	100
	1983	28	32	40	100
Liverpool	1977	38	28	34	100
	1983	34	27	39	100
Sheffield	1977	36	33	31	100
	1983	33	33	34	100
Leeds	1977	37	37	26	100
	1983	34	35	31	100

Source: CIPFA returns.

Table 8 Average outstanding debt per council dwelling,
Greater London, 1969–90, selected years

Year	Number of dwellings	Average debt per dwelling (£)
1969/70	537,237	3,223
1978/79	720,898	8,235
1989/90	307,024	17,845

Source: CIPFA Returns.

than halved between 1978/9 – the last full year before the 1980
Housing Act introduced the 'right to buy' – and the end of the 1980s.
Yet the outstanding debt per dwelling rose more than fivefold. And
this, it needs to be remembered, took place in a decade when rates of
investment in newbuild were extremely low, and when renovation
was heavily restricted by central government.

One reason for this astonishing lack of maturation is that central
government placed restrictions on the amount of capital receipts that
councils could access and use. Central government was concerned
that councils did not use their receipts to build new housing or renovate old housing too extensively. This makes calculation of the impact
of sales impossible from general summary statistics.

It is not even possible to obtain summary Department of Environment or CIPFA statistics covering the whole period that give average
Greater London newbuild prices, as the categories used have changed.
Sometimes costs are presented in terms of the value of tenders
approved – which gives no indication of final costs, sometimes selected
types of dwelling only are presented (for example, two-storey
five-bedroom houses), and sometimes land prices are not included in
costs.

Detailed empirical studies of the impact of discounted sales on costs
are urgently needed. These will need to be done based on the data
available from individual councils over the last couple of decades.
Until such basic data-collection is done and the results analysed by
researchers, our understanding of the impact of discounted sales on
maturation will remain virtually non-existent. The strong suspicion
must remain, however, that, based on what we know of the dynamics
of maturation, discounted sales retard or even in extreme cases reverse
the process of maturation.

7 Command policies

INTRODUCTION

Cost renting has often undergone a process of maturation under very specific historical political circumstances. For although cost renting can in theory be organised in many different ways, in practice it has been most commonly provided by the central or local state as a means of overcoming an acute housing shortage. Sometimes – though by no means always – this has been done as part of a socialist strategy of state control of key sectors of the economy. As already indicated, other forms of cost renting, such as rental co-operatives and cost rental trusts, have been less common, partly because socialist movements at a very early stage almost universally adopted statist strategies in preference to co-operative and mutual aid ones.

This historical contingency has been central in influencing the role and social organisation of cost renting. 'State provided' cost rental housing is very different in its aims and organisation from rental co-operatives or self-governing cost rental housing trusts. Its top-down paternalism comprises an organisational form that for much of the post-war period has been more or less acceptable to both paternalistic and authoritarian conservatism and state socialism. Concepts of grassroots participation and control on the housing market have been eclipsed by a concept of cost rental housing that is organised by the state and that is open to influence, in theory at least, via the electoral process rather than direct tenant participation, ownership or control.

State-owned and state-managed cost renting has therefore commonly been seen as a means of providing public rental housing that the private market has been unable to provide. Such politically controlled cost renting has always had a broad basis of support across the spectrum of political parties. Political control has provided the means to limit its scope to specific and often narrowly defined needs. For example, council housing in England has always had considerable support from rural conservatives partly because it provides a means of rehousing the retired occupants of the tied cottages of landowners so that new workers may be employed and housed. The form public renting has taken has therefore been the expression of an ideological rapprochement between reformist state socialism and Keynesian liberalism.

This meant that public renting came to be seen as supplementary to private profit renting rather than as an alternative to it, and was particularly heavily relied on to provide extra housing during the two decades immediately following the Second World War. This was needed to make up a huge backlog of housing brought about by the unusual combination which lasted for much of the preceding thirty years of a major economic depression sandwiched between two world wars. This specific role has in turn facilitated the ideological attacks on cost renting that have followed in the wake of the process of maturation and that has typically accompanied historic junctures emerging in the late post-war period.

In many countries, therefore, public rental housing expanded dramatically during the early post-war decades. The tensions inherent in the status of cost renting as a supplement to private renting did not cause problems so long as there was a broadly agreed need for supplementary rental housing to alleviate the most acute shortages, and as long as the public rental sector did not become too large or undercut private rents too heavily. However, the process of maturation of cost renting involves a socio-economic dynamic that ultimately brings the tensions inherent in the social organisation of an essentially supplementary cost rental sector to the surface and compels resolution one way or the other.

How and when this crisis management took place varied considerably from country to country. In New Zealand it took place at a very early stage because of the manner in which public renting had been rapidly increased during the immediate post-war years while rents were frozen. In Australia it took place considerably later, in the late 1970s. In Britain, after a false start in the early 1970s it took place in the early 1980s and did so in a much more acute form. The discussion below brings out these differences, after which their main outlines are summarised and some conclusions drawn.

NEW ZEALAND[1]

The rise of state housing in New Zealand coincides with the period of Labour government from 1935 to 1949. The labour government had an ambitious housing programme, aimed at creating a substantial state rental sector. During this period there was a dramatic expansion of state rental housing. According to Davidson (1992) by 1940, 45 per cent of new construction was state-built housing and, at its peak, state rental housing accounted for almost 20 per cent of the stock.

The new housing policy was two tiered. The first tier was intended as support for the least well off members of society in the form of state rental housing. A second-tier based on substantial subsidies for new owner occupied housing was intended for those who could afford to buy if they received initial help. The first tier was a new innovation intended to supplement the existing assistance for access to owner occupation, and was the major change in housing policy introduced by the Labour government.

The rapid expansion of state housing was a clear indication that the definition of the least well off members of society was a broad one. It contrasts markedly with the much more residual housing policy ambitions in other English-speaking settler societies. In the USA, Canada and Australia – and later in New Zealand, too – the public rental housing stock accounted for 5 per cent or less of the total stock.

Yet despite the generous definition of need implied by the New Zealand building programme the policy remained one wed to the concept that cost rental housing was residual. No attempt was ever made to develop cost renting into a general-access form of tenure. Nor was any attempt ever made to integrate state rental housing with private rental housing. Rental policy was therefore clearly dualist in strategy.

Originally, New Zealand's state rental housing was intended to be cost-covering. That is, rents were intended to cover debt-servicing and running costs as well as the creation of funds for structural repairs, renovation and modernisation. It was even envisaged that a modest surplus could be made.

However, there was no systematic rent policy devised, and this proved ultimately to be the undoing of New Zealand state rental housing. Rents were more or less pegged so that their value fell in real terms quite substantially in just a few years to well below costs. The rapid – not to say dramatic – expansion of the stock during the

first decade of the programme leading up to the end of the war must
have meant that little or no maturation had taken place since the
beginning of the programme.

At the end of the war, as the economy reverted to peacetime
conditions, acute housing shortages resulted in a construction boom.
In just a few years construction prices first doubled and then trebled.
Since state housing constructions also increased during this period to
attempt to satisfy the growing demand, little or no maturation of the
stock can therefore have taken place after the war. Yet rents
remained pegged and by the late 1940s were about half that of rents
in the private sector. Already in 1944 the low rents were attracting
a strong demand for public rental housing, reflected in a waiting list
of 30,000 households.

This inevitably attracted National Party and conservative media
attacks on 'the subsidised state tenant' and 'what it costs you to provide the other fellow's house'. The National Party won the 1949
general election on a platform of dismantling state controls. This
included the sale of state housing, a measure which won considerable
electoral support among state tenants.

The coming to office of the National government proved to be
decisive for the future of the state rental housing sector. The government embarked on a major programme of sales of state housing
to sitting tenants. In 1951 2,904 state houses were built while in the
same year 4,001 state houses were sold to tenants. By the 1970s state
housing's share of the total housing stock had fallen to 5 per cent
before stabilising.

The New Zealand sales programme is notable because, on government admission (New Zealand, 1953), at least some of the housing
sold was sold at a price below construction cost. This is understandable since the state housing stock was very immature and wholesale
asset stripping on the scale that was envisaged may well have been
difficult to achieve otherwise.

It is a measure of the unquestioned nature of the new policy strategy
that no media indignation over 'double subsidies' ensued from this
issue. The very same 'subsidised state tenants' who were decried in the
1949 general election campaign were now being given an additional
subsidy to buy their houses. This kind of double standard when talking
about subsidies to public tenants is quite common. It must throw
considerable doubt on how genuine such indignation is and raise questions about the extent to which the hubris is merely a smokescreen
behind which attacks to undermine public rental housing can be
launched.

The New Zealand example is also interesting because it demonstrates the importance of developing a rent policy that makes economic sense. This is not to say that it need not involve subsidies; it often has to when setting up a new cost rental sector. The original policy was clearly cost based, but then rents were not raised in step with increasing costs. This exposed the policy to attack by the way in which it provoked a rent-differential crisis.

It might be mentioned here that a similar problem, though on a much larger scale, confronts post-communist countries wishing to establish a dualist rental system. Decades of rent setting that bear no relation to either costs or demand combined with massive neglect of maintenance and modernisation have left most of these countries with a stock that needs major restructuring. In some countries the neglect of the fabric of the buildings has been so great that it is even difficult to sell to sitting tenants without giving the flats away, or in extreme cases paying tenants to take them off the hands of the state. The New Zealand situation, after only fifteen years of large-scale construction, showed all the early symptoms of this problem.

AUSTRALIA[2]

Like New Zealand, Australian housing policy underwent an early post-war reorientation that proved to be only temporary. During the late 1940s the Labor federal government attempted to develop a public cost rental sector as a complement to the subsidisation of owner occupation. As in New Zealand, this was attacked ferociously by the National Party and was a factor in the defeat of Labor and the entrenchment of a dualist rental system during the 1950s and 1960s. That historic juncture has many features in common with that in New Zealand and has been discussed elsewhere (see Kemeny, 1983a, pp. 9–16). For that reason it will not be dealt with here. Instead, I propose to examine a rent-differential crisis that emerged in Australia during the 1970s, and that resulted in the introduction of 'market rents', the impact of which has been examined in the preceding chapter.

The tension between the desire to keep cost renting as a small residualised sector and the demand pressures caused by the maturation process can be clearly seen in the case of Australian public renting. Public renting in Australia has always been provided by the states, usually through a State Housing Commission which has a monopoly of public rental housing in the state. Federal support has been provided in recent decades through periodically re-negotiated

Commonwealth–State Housing Agreements (CSHAs) by which low-interest loans were provided for the construction of new rental housing.

Public renting had been envisaged from an early stage in most states as a supplementary form of housing. As such, it was subject to stringent expansion restrictions. These were effectively imposed on the states by the federal government by virtue of the amount of loan monies provided. So even when state governments were elected that wished to expand public renting, and were prepared to invest in doing so, their limited resources made it difficult to overcome the limitations of CSHA finance effectively.

In addition, heavy asset stripping since the early 1950s through discounted sales to sitting tenants was pursued by most states with more or less enthusiasm depending on which political party was in state government, though, as we have seen in the previous chapter, South Australia was an exception. So the combination of severe federal limitations on the funding of a popular form of rental housing and extensive and sustained asset stripping kept the public rental sector in most states below 5 per cent of the housing stock.

This two-pronged strategy successfully held down the size of the national public rental stock to around 5 per cent of dwellings. An early rapid post-war expansion of public renting such as took place in New Zealand never materialised due to the short tenure of the federal Labor government. By the 1960s, with dualism firmly established, even the federal Labor Party had come to see the role of public renting as strictly residual, and adopted the dualist terminology of referring to public renting as 'welfare housing', while not applying this label also to the heavily subsidised owner occupier market.

Australian public housing is highly centralised in its organisation. Since Australia has a federal political system, each state is responsible for its own public rental housing, and so there is only one public rental housing commission for each of the six states. Each commission will therefore own thousands or even tens of thousands of dwellings scattered over towns and settlements which can be hundreds of miles apart.

As we have seen, the South Australian Housing Trust has, alone of the states, steadfastly refused from the very start to engage in large-scale asset stripping through discounted sales and as a result its stock of housing has attained a considerably higher level of maturation than in the other states. Despite this, the attitude towards public renting in South Australia remained in accord with that elsewhere in Australia: that public renting was an essentially residual and supplementary form of housing. In 1962 the Premier of South Australia put the case for a command policy in unusually frank and brutal terms, revealing the authoritarian ulterior motives that lay behind such a policy:

> We do not want to make [rental] housing more attractive to the detriment of home ownership. Home ownership is what we strive to foster. If you allow people with big incomes to rent houses at attractive rents they will never buy.
>
> (cited in Jones, 1972, p. 24)

The strategy of discounted sales succeeded in delaying the maturation process of the national public rental housing stock taken as a whole. Sales at times amounted to more than the numbers built, and often exceeded 50 per cent of new construction rates. This was particularly so in the two most populous states of New South Wales and Victoria, where vigorous sales policies with generous subsidies in the form of discounted prices and favourable mortgage terms were granted.

The early decades of the post-war period were a time of rapid urbanisation of Australia. This took the form of extensive suburbanisation as, with the predominance of the detached house and the spread of car ownership, urban sprawl made Australian cities among those of the lowest density in the world. One consequence of this was that as the urbanisation process took place, the distribution of the public rental stock in the larger cities began to take on a 'doughnut' shape. New constructions were placed in the expanding suburbs, while sales of existing stock, first in the inner city areas and then increasingly in the inner suburbs first eroded then virtually eliminated the stock of public rental housing in those areas.

However, levels of sales were insufficiently high and the size of discounts were insufficiently large to neutralise the maturation process entirely. In particular, the public rental stock was subject to maturation created by rising prices. Thus, rapid house price inflation during the early 1970s reduced public rents in Australia as a whole from 90 per cent of the level of private rents in 1966 to only 53 per cent in 1976. In just one decade, then, public rents had fallen from near parity with private rents to well below them.

The appointment of a conservative government following the 1975 coup d'état[3] and the opportunity in 1978 to negotiate a new Commonwealth–State Housing Agreement determining federal subsidy levels for public renting therefore combined to create a historic juncture to facilitate the expeditious solving of the impending rent-differential crisis in Australian public rental housing.

This agreement introduced the concept of 'market rents' in public renting, whereby above cost-covering rents would be charged and the surpluses made as a result of this would be clawed back by the federal government. Since then, there has been a long period of Labor Party government and the concept of market rents has been quietly dropped. However, as we have seen, rents remain considerably higher than costs and there has been no change under Labor in the fundamental approach to the role of public renting, which retains its essentially 'welfare housing' role. Should a government more hostile to public renting take office we may expect a resurgence of federal attempts to push rents up and to claw back surpluses thereby generated. A period of rapid house price inflation may well provide the trigger for a new rent-differential crisis to materialise.

The major lesson to be learned from the Australian experience is that even in a country with a well established dualist rental system, the maturation of the public rental sector can result in the emergence of a rent-differential crisis. Rent-differential crises are therefore not simply a one-off hurdle that the proponents of a dualist strategy policy must overcome, after which the dualist system simply continues smoothly on its course. Rather, the maturation process can – and often does – lead to recurring rent-differential crises that require repeated periodic major intervention by central government which increasingly leads to the establishment of a command economy.

BRITAIN

The situation in Britain differs from that in both New Zealand and Australia because in Britain the public rental sector was allowed to expand to a much more significant proportion of the housing stock. By the 1960s council housing was in the almost unique situation of any cost rental housing stock in the world of being both the major form of rental housing provision accounting for nearly a third of the total housing stock and being relatively mature with about a third of council housing being pre-war.

Malpass (1990) argues that the policy assault on council housing began after the deregulation of private renting in the mid-1960s increased private rents significantly above council rents. The situation was probably aggravated because the Labour government of the late 1960s held council rents artificially low as a counter-inflation device (Cooper, 1985, p. 19).

Thus, in contrast to the Australian situation, it was not the maturation of council housing per se that led to its suddenly increased competitiveness. It was rather the deregulation of private renting that resulted in the already considerably mature council housing beginning to significantly undercut rapidly rising private rents in a very short period of time. The British rent-differential crisis was therefore an unintended consequence of the deregulation of private rents.

It was for this reason that it was only in the mid-1960s that political opposition to the maturation process in council housing began to take shape. The spate of media spleen over council tenants with two cars that was a particular feature of this period was not produced by some sudden and inexplicable fall in council rents but by the relative cheapness of council rents compared to private rents. The solution to this 'problem' took the form of Conservative Party plans to force councils to charge above cost-covering rents and thereby negate the competitive edge of council housing. The Conservative Party was in opposition at this time, and so it was only in 1970 when it took office that the conditions combined to create a historic juncture.

The 1972 legislation to compel councils to charge surplus-generating 'fair rents' was an explicit attempt to re-establish parity between private and public renting. The system of 'fair rents' was already in place and applied to certain forms of private renting. It attempted to provide private landlords with what were considered reasonable margins of profit without allowing them to benefit from scarcity.

Fair rents were also applied to housing associations, a new form of non-profit rental housing that was emerging in Britain at the time. However, fair rents did not generate surpluses for housing associations since they were a new form of rental provision with relatively immature stocks of housing.

The implementation of fair rents in council housing would have eliminated most, if not all, of the state subsidy to council housing and established council housing on a similar footing in terms of rents and subsidies to private renting. It would also have given all three forms of rental provision – private, housing association and council – the same system of rent setting.

It is possible to argue that the introduction of fair rents in council housing could be seen as an attempt to create a unitary rental market. It is also possible to argue that the choice of fair rents as the common rent-setting system indicates that the kind of unitary rental market that would have resulted would have been based on 'part-profit' principles. This is because the fair rent system was based on the principle that landlords should be able to make 'reasonable' profits but should not be able to benefit from high rents caused by housing scarcity.

However, there was no explicit – or for that matter implicit – argument in these terms. And since the measure was only in effect for a few years before being repealed by the next government, it is more likely that the Conservative government was more narrowly concerned with reducing council housing subsidies and raising rents to dampen demand and thereby shorten waiting lists. Attributing to this policy a broad strategic vision that broke with traditional dualist principles is therefore almost certainly unjustified.

The Labour government of 1974–9 repealed the fair rents legislation, but otherwise retained the prior status quo and did nothing to move council housing towards a unitary rental market. The 1977 Green Paper on housing (Harloe, 1978) failed to address this issue and reflected the ideological bankruptcy of the Labour Party in terms of rental housing policy that was to have fatal consequences for council housing. The early 1970s had witnessed a very dramatic increase in house prices, which had the effect of further accelerating the maturation of council housing (by decreasing the ratio of new to existing council housing debt). At the same time more radical policies were being developed in the Conservative party.

With the appointment of a new Conservative government in 1979 the conditions were once again favourable for the emergence of a historic juncture. This time there was no attempt to re-introduce fair rents in council housing. Instead, the 1980 Housing Act gave the minister responsible for housing sweeping new powers to reduce subsidies. This was achieved by changing the subsidy system such that each year the central government would assume an average national level of rent increases and on the basis of that assumption reduce subsidy accordingly.

This quickly reduced subsidies in an increasing number of councils to zero. It also increasingly produced net surpluses on council housing revenue accounts which could in theory be clawed back by central government in the form of negative subsidies (implicit taxation). Central government did this by applying a two-stage logic.

It was first assumed that the council housing surpluses made even when council housing was no longer in receipt of any subsidies at all would be transferred to the local general rate fund. Central government then reduced its general subsidy to local government for non-housing activities on a *pro rata* basis. That is, the assumption was made that surpluses made on council housing would be used to subsidise the rates which would in turn reduce the need for general rate support. These measures substantially increased central government control over council housing and were successful in forcing rents up and subsidies down.

At the same time legislation was passed compelling councils to sell to sitting tenants who wished to buy (the so-called 'right to buy') – and even to sell to other landlords who wished to buy under certain prescribed circumstances – at prices well below market levels and centralising the power to arbitrate final appeals in the hands of the secretary of state responsible for housing to exercise personal discretion and to decide outcomes by fiat. Council newbuild was also severely restricted by limiting council borrowing for council housing investment.

The government's new rent and subsidy policy contributed significantly to the success of the right to buy by supplementing the carrot of subsidies in the form of heavily discounted sale prices with the stick of rapidly rising rents. However, the new system had weaknesses and above all loopholes which councils could exploit. In particular, although councils retained the possibility of subsidising local taxpayers from council housing surpluses by transferring housing revenue account surpluses to the general rate fund, they also retained the possibility of cross-subsidising in the opposite direction.

This effectively meant that councils could avoid raising rents by replacing lost central government subsidy on the housing revenue account with a transfer from the general rate fund. In addition, the blanket national rent increases which central government decreed would be the basis for calculating subsidies each year was too insensitive to local variations.

The system was therefore changed in the 1989 Local Government and Housing Act by which the government further extended its control over council housing (Malpass *et al.*, 1993). It did this by a number of measures.

In the first place, instead of using some notional nationwide data about rents and subsidies, the government collected large amounts of data on council housing from councils and used this to derive assumptions specific to each individual council about average local levels of rent and managerial cost increases. These assessments in turn were used as the basis for determining levels of subsidy.

Subsidies were therefore reduced on the basis of assumptions made by central government about the level of rents that each individual council would charge in the coming year, rather than some average notional rent level for the whole country. This enabled government to influence individual council rent setting, while not directly challenging councils' fiercely defended – though by now only nominal – right to set rents themselves.

An important innovation of the 1989 Act was to include central government rent rebates in the general housing subsidy. Rapidly rising rents and falling subsidies together with the increasing residualisation of council housing as the better-off tenants exercised the right to buy had meant that rent rebates increasingly replaced general housing subsidies as the main form of central government support to council tenants.

Since general council housing subsidies were rapidly disappearing, merging general housing subsidies and rent rebates opened up the possibility that some of the cost of rent rebates could be paid for by housing revenue account surpluses. This would relieve the social security burden of many of the poorer tenants by passing on the cost of supporting them to those council tenants who could afford the higher rents.

Councils were also forbidden to transfer money in either direction between the housing revenue account and the general local government budget except when the housing revenue account was in surplus and when directed to transfer this surplus to the general rate fund by central government. This enabled central government to control how much money was transferred and when, and gave it more control over local budgets and subsidies to local budgets. Government also tightened its control over local borrowing to prevent councils from raising loans on non-housing assets in order to finance council housing newbuild and renovation.

Finally, we may note that government placed further restrictions on the ways in which councils could use the capital receipts from council house sales. Most important, they could not be used to build new council housing or to renovate existing stock. They had to be used to reduce the outstanding debt on existing stock. The intention behind this seems to be both to head off any attempt at meeting the enormous backlog of demand for council housing while at the same time ensuring that by further reducing the debt-servicing cost of council housing larger surpluses would be increasingly made which central government could then claw back and dispose of.

There are already a few councils where the income from rents – net of debt-servicing and other costs – is so great that they are able to cover the costs of rent rebates, thereby relieving the central government social security budget of this cost, and still leave a surplus over for compulsory transfer to the general rate fund, which central government can then use to offset from, and thereby reduce, its general local government grant support.

Malpass *et al.* (1993, p. 86) illustrate this with the case of a council, St Edmondsbury in Lincolnshire. In 1990/1 the council received total net subsidy on its stock of just under 8,000 dwellings of £71,463 or about £9 per dwelling. However, it had paid rent rebates out of rent receipts totalling £3 millions, implying a total negative subsidy of just over £2.9 millions or a negative subsidy (implicit tax) per tenant of over £370 in that year.[4] In 1991/2 total net subsidies were minus £319,000, or an implicit tax per council tenant of over £40. Because the housing revenue account was in net surplus, that surplus was compulsorily transferred to the general rate fund. But with rent rebates of £3.1 millions total net negative subsidies in that year were £3,419,000 (£3.1 millions rent rebates plus £319,000 net negative subsidy) or £435 per tenant. Estimates for 1992/3 show a doubling of the net negative subsidy to £650,000.

The 1989 Act significantly increased central government control over council housing, allowing it to push rents up and subsidies down and to cream off council housing surpluses to the central exchequer. The measures combined both to undermine maturation while preventing its expansion and to residualise council housing, keeping it clearly separated from the private rental market.

CONCLUSIONS

The British case is interesting because it represents an example of the implementation of a particularly draconian command policy in order to destabilise and undermine an already large and mature public rental housing stock. This marks Britain off from most other English-speaking countries in which the public rental sector was not allowed to expand so dramatically in the first place.

The policy pursued by the British government during the 1980s has many elements in common with the Australian system. There, too, discounted sales, surplus-generating rents, and using such surpluses to pay housing allowances comprised a package of measures to suppress public renting. Surplus-generating rents, council house sales and shifting the burden of housing allowances from the national social security budget to tenants may well have been inspired directly by the Australian experience. Certainly, Thatcher visited Australia shortly before becoming prime minister and had been impressed by Australian housing policy.

Yet, despite heavy state suppression of public renting in Australia throughout the 1950s, 1960s, and early 1970s a rent-differential crisis still emerged by the mid-1970s. And to the extent that the maturation of council housing was greatly accelerated during the middle years of the post-war period as a result of house price inflation, the British experience parallels that of Australia. There has been a need to tighten up on central government control throughout the decade, and there is no reason to believe that the end of the process is in sight.

As others have already observed (Murie, 1993, p. 156) the 1980s witnessed a perceptible shift in strategic managerial control of council housing from councils to central government. It thereby entrenched more deeply the command policy that is an integral part of rent-differential crisis management.

Another point worth noting is that because British council housing is so mature, special circumstances pertain to the British case. Maturation is more advanced than in any other country and is in fact so advanced in many local authorities that it is increasingly possible to make a substantial surplus on council housing revenue accounts.

This has clearly been a major motivation for central government to tighten its control over rent levels and the manner in which surpluses are disposed of. Ideally, government will want to ensure that all housing allowances are paid for out of the rents of the less poor tenants rather than out of the national social security budget. Over and above this, rents will hopefully be sufficiently high on a stock of dwellings that has very low debt-servicing charges that surpluses can be made on the revenue accounts that can be creamed off into the central exchequer.

The main limitation on this is, of course, the residualisation policy pursued through council house sales and shortage-induced restricted access. As a larger and larger proportion of tenants require rent rebates, the surplus-generating capacity of the stock falls. There may well be an interesting cyclical dynamic involved here that is worthy of conceptual development and further investigation between rising rents, rising proportions of rent rebate recipients and falling net rental surpluses.

That the state suppression of public renting is not a once-and-for-all act is clear from the Australian case. More important, the British experience demonstrates that in a less centralised public rental system such as that in Britain, a process of centralisation takes place in spurts and starts whenever rent-differential crises require to be managed. It is one thing to exert central government control over six public housing authorities as in Australia, but quite another in Britain where hundreds of councils are involved. Constant vigilance is needed to ensure that the public rental housing stock does not mature and begin once again to edge demand for public rental housing upwards.

Rent-differential crises are, therefore, a recurring phenomenon and an integral part of state measures to sustain a dualist rental system. They are the basic reason why a command economy is needed as a growing and permanent feature of the management of public renting to keep it as a residual and marginal form of tenure.

Despite this, the possibility of a more radical shift of policy strategy always remains tantalisingly on the horizon. The fair rents legislation, for example, could have marked the introduction of a unitary policy had the other principles of a unitary market strategic policy been introduced. The line between measures that entrench dualism and measures that tip a dualist system over in the direction of developing into a unitary rental market is a fine one. What distinguishes them from one another is more the cumulative impact of a package of measures taken together. It is therefore *policy strategy* that ultimately determines the nature of the rental system a country possesses.

In Chapter 10, when examining how a strategic policy shift might be made from dualism to a unitary market, we will see that similar possibilities have emerged in more recent years, as an unintended consequence of an attempt to suppress council housing by countering its maturation benefits. Both these attempts to solve a rent-differential crisis indicate how, with just a relatively modest shift in emphasis it is possible to swing an entire rental system from dualism to unitarism, or, indeed, in the other direction. The social construction of a rental system is evidently a fragile and sensitive process.

8 Market policies

INTRODUCTION

Countries which are developing unitary rental markets possess large rental markets, accounting for between 40 and 70 per cent of the total housing stock, compared to between 20 and 40 per cent in dualist rental systems. In addition, the cost and profit rental stocks are not segregated off from one another into different forms of tenure as they are in English-speaking countries. Instead, 'renting' is one form of tenure even if there are variations in forms of provision, mostly between different categories of owner. In general there are therefore no fundamental tenure cleavages between rental housing owned by different kinds of landlords.

On the other hand, cost rental housing may display a much wider variety of forms than is normally the case in a dualist system. These may range from public renting through semi-autonomous non-profit trusts to co-operative rental associations. A number of in-between forms may also exist, such as limited-profit companies and housing companies that are only non-profit because their owners – whether the local authority or some organisation such as a trades union – want them to be. In some countries one type of cost rental housing may predominate, while in others there may be a more evenly balanced mix of a wide range of types.

Different strategies may also be adopted towards the balance between cost renting of all kinds and profit renting. Profit renting may be simply allowed to be squeezed out by cost renting, or, alternatively, it may be sustained through subsidisation. In fact, most countries seem to have encouraged privately owned profit renting to continue to play a part on the rental market. This may reflect the role of private landlords in corporatist policy making. It may equally reflect the basic philosophy behind market solutions, which is that the more diversity and competition there is the better.

Finally and crucially, the manner in which harmonisation is attained – or rather moved towards – may vary greatly. For although the basic principle – that cost rental should be allowed to compete with profit renting and thereby hold rents down – is a major distinguishing characteristic of unitary rental markets, it may be implemented in many different ways.

The following case studies illustrate the diversity of solutions that have been adopted. Indeed, no two societies among those identified so far as pursuing a unitary rental strategy have taken the same route to achieving it. Moreover, the solutions adopted vary so greatly that they sometimes appear to have little in common with one another except the basic principle of creating an integrated rental market with a substantial element of cost-determination in market rent levels. Countries with unitary rental market strategies therefore demonstrate a richness of variety that is strikingly absent from countries which have adopted a dualist strategy.

The variety of approaches to developing a unitary rental market and the distinctiveness of each country comes out clearly in the following case studies. Following the presentation of the case studies I attempt, in Chapter 9, to formulate some general principles to explain the differences found.

SWEDEN

The move towards an integrated public–private rental sector began in Sweden in response to the massive flight of investment from housing to war industries that took place after the outbreak of the Second World War. The implicit deal that was offered to private landlords in 1942 was that they would be eligible for subsidised state housing loans in return for which they would have to accept the same rent regulations and offer comparable housing standards and security of tenure as the cost rental housing companies. The rent-setting system that was introduced was one of rent regulation based on the principle of covering the incurred historic capital costs of individual rental buildings plus running, maintenance, administration and other costs.

This system remained in force for a quarter of a century. During that time, because of inflation, rents of older dwellings rose more slowly than those of newer dwellings. This created increasingly acute distortions in demand as older cheaper flats became more sought after than newer more expensive ones. During this period, too, the stocks of cost rental housing companies expanded dramatically. By the mid-1960s the rental market was composed of about equal proportions of privately owned and cost rental housing company owned housing. However, as the Swedish case study in Chapter 6 indicates, cost rental housing was considerably less mature than private renting.

The rent-setting system that is in force today was first established in 1968 when the use-value principle was extended from the cost rental housing companies (to which it had been applied since the late 1950s) to private rental housing and when the current rent-setting machinery was established. The intention was to move away from individual historic cost regulated rents towards a form of unregulated rents negotiated between the main parties on the rental market.

The guiding principle of this system was that cost rental housing company rents should reflect use-values but without violating the no-profit principle. This meant in practice that the cost rental housing companies would charge above cost-covering rents on those dwellings in their stock that had high use-value but low costs, and use the surplus to lower the rents of those dwellings in their stock that had high costs but low use-value.

What was novel about this system was that the demand-sensitive pooled rents arrived at in the cost rental housing company stock were to be used as guidelines in determining the rents of all the stock including those owned by private landlords. In other words, the cost rental housing companies were to become 'market leaders' in determining rent levels for the rental market as a whole.

The procedure that was chosen for setting the rents of cost rental housing companies was not left, as it is in unregulated markets, to administrative decree by housing company executives. Instead it was based on negotiations between local tenants unions and cost rental housing companies within guidelines negotiated on the national level between the umbrella organisation of the cost rental housing companies (SABO) and the National Federation of Tenants Unions. In addition there were special local authority – and cross-local authority – harmonisation procedures, tenants union and private landlord association negotiations over private rents, and a complex appeal and review system.

For various reasons, including resistance by the Tenants Union during the annual negotiations, the new rent-setting system did not lead to the introduction of fully demand-sensitive rents. As subsequent research revealed, a strong element of individual historic costs remained (Bergenstråhle, 1982; Turner, 1979, 1983). This was most clearly evident in that during periods of surplus housing it was generally the newer, higher-rent, housing where vacancy rates were the highest. With fully demand-sensitive rents, vacancies might be expected to be more randomly distributed in the stock.

The failure to move completely from individual historic costs to use-value rents that were based on cost rental housing company pooled costs has had both advantages and disadvantages. Its advantage has been that the delay has allowed cost rental housing company housing stocks to mature.

The advantage of the delay derives from the fact that when use-value rents were introduced the cost rental housing was still very immature. Cost rental housing companies had spent the period from the mid-1940s to the mid-1970s rapidly expanding their stocks. This period, as we have seen in the case of Gavlegårdarna, was therefore one of heavy front loading. So when use-value rents were introduced in 1968 the cost rental housing company stock was almost as large as the private rental stock but its cost structure was much higher.

Introducing use-value rents at that time would therefore have resulted in a high rate of profit extraction by private landlords. Since the mid-1970s the rate of cost rental housing company newbuild has declined dramatically, allowing the cost structure of the cost rental housing company stock to mature rapidly. At the same time, extensive (state subsidised) modernisation programmes have increased the indebtedness of the privately owned stock.

The disadvantage of the delay in moving towards harmonisation has been that a continuing large element of individual historic costs in rents has been perpetuated and has exacerbated the skewing of demand for rental housing. This has in turn increased the political opposition to the existing system. There have been increasing calls for a freer and more market harmonised rent-setting system over the last decade or so.

The coming to office of a right of centre coalition government in 1991 was the first right of centre government since those of 1976–82. The Social Democrats had held office continually since the eary 1930s other than these two periods. The 1976–82 governments made no major changes to the rental market. The more recent government has had a much more interventionist approach to the rental market, with plans for privatisation in a number of important respects. Their policies are likely to result in a number of important changes to the rent-setting system, freeing it up considerably.

At time of writing, these plans for reform have not been finalised, let alone the necessary legislation passed. One possibility that is being discussed is to remove the negotiation role of the tenants union, allowing cost rental housing companies to determine their own rents.

It is not yet clear whether the removal of this watch-dog role would result in higher rents. In theory this might be what one would predict.

It could be argued that cost rental companies have no market incentive to minimise costs, while tenants clearly do. So having tenants unions negotiate annual rent increases may be one way of ensuring that costs are kept to a minimum. In practice, the tenants union influence has been on the distribution of rents – and therefore costs – across the whole stock. Because it is only engaged in annual rent increase negotiations it is not really in a position to influence the costs that are incurred throughout the year.

An arguably more important change has been that cost rental housing companies may no longer act as official market leaders for the private rental stock. In future, rents will be considered reasonable if they do not substantially exceed those of comparable housing. This loosening up of the rent-setting system can be expected to result in considerable increases in private rents, at least in the medium run.[1] Eventually, however, it is likely that cost rental housing companies will move into the market for older – still largely privately owned – rental stock and as they build these up will be in a better position to influence rents there too.

The Swedish rental market is currently undergoing changes which are fully in line with the continued development of a unitary rental market. As yet there are no signs that the government intends a frontal assault on cost renting. Even the sale of cost rental flats to tenants is not being pursued in such a manner as to force cost rental housing companies to sell at loss-making discounts. Without such discounts sales are likely to remain modest in the extreme. Nor are there any plans to force cost rental housing companies to privatise, for example by conversion into joint-stock companies. Such changes would constitute clear signals of an intention to abandon unitary renting for a dualist system in which the cost rental housing is residualised and its role limited to housing largely disadvantaged groups.

It is therefore safe to say that so far the rent differentials between cost and profit renting in Sweden have led to modest harmonisation attempts. They have not led to anything that can be discerned as a historic juncture between a rent-differential crisis and a government hostile to the principle of a unitary rental market.

THE NETHERLANDS

The Netherlands has a large rental market, comprising 60 per cent of the total national stock of housing of which over two-thirds are owned by cost rental housing organisations. These are mainly organised along ethnic and religious regional lines. There is also some local authority provided rental housing, though little has been built since 1967.

The bulk of rental housing is therefore cost rental, although subsidies are available to private landlords as well. The rent-setting system produces what is termed a 'dynamic cost price rent' based on current actually incurred costs while subsidies further reduce this to a 'demand rent' being the amount actually paid by the households (see Brouwer, 1988; Klunder, 1988).

Since 1988 state loans have been withdrawn and finance must be found on the market. This reflects the fact that the maturation of the stock has proceeded sufficiently far to progress the withdrawal of subsidies to a significant extent even if substantial subsidies still remain. It would therefore seem that the Dutch rental market is beginning the transition from rent regulation to unregulated rents that a relatively mature cost rental market makes possible.

What is particularly striking about the Dutch approach is the great preponderance of cost rental over profit rental housing. The strategy here seems to be quite different from that in Sweden where private landlords still own nearly half of the rental stock. In Sweden, as we have noted, there have been, and remain, substantial harmonisation problems between private and cost rents. These have been largely avoided in The Netherlands because of the great preponderance of cost rental housing on the rental market as a whole.

GERMANY

Germany has pursued a quite different strategy from that of either Sweden or The Netherlands. Approximately 60 per cent of the (West) German[2] housing stock is rental housing, of which some 10 per cent are owned by non-profit housing companies, and a further 7 per cent by tenant co-operatives. The percentage of the total rental stock that is cost rental in organisation – that is, whose owners are explicitly non-profit in orientation – is therefore fairly modest, with the bulk of rental housing being owned by profit-orientated landlords.

On the face of it, then, Germany possesses a rental market that is not too different from that in Britain, with only a slightly smaller cost rental stock than the council housing stock. This is deceptive, however. Closer examination reveals that rents are kept to near cost rental levels by a unique two-tier rent regulation system.

The first of these is similar to the Swedish system of rent regulation tied to the granting of public subsidies to both non-profit and profit-orientated landlords. The rent and subsidy system is organised in such a way that 25-year subsidies[3] are available to all landlords of newly constructed housing in return for which rents are kept at cost-covering levels during that period. After the first 25 years of such a building's life the subsidies are withdrawn and rent regulation is removed. This first tier of rent regulation therefore comprises most rental dwellings built within the previous 25 years. The size and composition of this stock will therefore vary over time depending on rates of new-build by different kinds of landlord.

The second tier of rent regulation applies to all other rental housing: i.e. housing neither owned by cost rental housing organisations nor subject to subsidy-related rent regulation. Andersen *et al.* (1992, p. 70) estimate this to amount to 44 per cent of the stock. This second phase of rent regulation has a number of components (Andersen *et al.*, 1992, pp. 70–88), the most important of which ties rent increases to a level that does not significantly exceed local rent levels. Vacant rental dwellings may not be subject to rent increases that exceed the local rent level by more than 20 per cent. For existing tenancies, rents cannot be raised more than 30 per cent above the local rent levels over a three-year period, nor raised more than once a year.

Local rent levels for different sizes and standards of dwellings must by law be determined annually by all local authorities with a population of over 15,000. This so-called *Mietspiegel* (literally 'mirror rent') attempts to accurately reflect local rent levels, and so can be described as *marktkonform*, in accordance with social market principles. The larger local authorities have based these on statistics and studies by research institutes, while the smaller local authorities have tended to use more informal methods of estimating the local mirror rent.

Landlords can raise rents either with reference to increases in the local mirror rent level for the appropriate type of dwelling, or if at least three similar dwellings in the landlord's stock have rent levels similar to that proposed by the landlord, or if a public rent assessor fixes a higher rent for the dwelling in question. Security of tenure legislation ensures that eviction notice can only be given if the tenant has not fulfilled contractual duties, if the owner or a near relative of the owner intends to live in the dwelling, or if the dwelling is to be used for other purposes (major renovation being defined as one such).

The net effect of the German system is that the combined market weight of cost rental housing organisations plus the first-tier regulated/ subsidised profit-orientated rental housing plus the downward pull on rents exerted by the second tier of rent regulation operate to hold down market rents. Andersen *et al.* (1992, p. 75, Figure 4.1) show that the resulting rent pattern in Germany includes an element of individual historic costs, with the rents in 1986/7 of dwellings built before 1940 having rents in general less than 75 per cent of those built in 1986/7.

The uniqueness of the German system lies in the existence of a substantial pool of housing owned by both cost rental and subsidised profit-orientated landlords but all charging cost-covering rents, while as housing ages and moves out of subsidy it also moves out of the cost-covering rent regime and into the much looser second-tier rent regulation system. It is therefore not possible to establish with any degree of precision the number of dwellings that are cost covering at any point in time. The difficulty in identifying which landlords are profit-orientated and which are cost rental orientated is therefore a central feature of the German rental market.

Leutner and Jensen (1988, p. 166) estimate that in 1982 30 per cent of the rental stock was subsidised (and hence regulated). More recently, Haeussermann (1991) conservatively estimates the total cost-covering rental stock (i.e. both cost rental housing and first-tier rent regulated profit-orientated landlords) at 26 per cent of the total rental housing stock, though of course there will be wide local variations: in many urban areas considerably more (Hamburg being notably exceptional with around 50 per cent) and in rural areas considerably less.

This stock covers a range of dwelling types and age, including new and recently built housing owned by profit-orientated landlords and the entire stocks of cost rental housing companies and rental co-operatives. These effectively provide the yardstick by which rents of 'unregulated' housing can be set in the looser and more flexible comparison-based 'second tier' of rent regulation.

Here, then, we have a different route to a unitary rental market from that in either Sweden or The Netherlands. The system would appear to be deliberately one of de-institutionalising different forms of ownership and subsidised and unsubsidised housing to create a diversity and complexity that defies simplistic categorisation and that therefore hinders the emergence of clearly defined rental sub-sectors, ghettoisation and residualisation. The German rental market therefore follows closely the prescription of ordo-liberals that markets have a diversity of suppliers, that they minimise the need for a safety-net social security system, and that pricing be market determined, though within bounds set by the state.

The finesse in the system is that cost rental housing comprises a substantial pool of low-rent housing to dampen rents in general, and that this stock of housing automatically renews itself as older, low-debt, housing – both 'private' and 'public' – passes out of subsidy and therefore out of rent regulation while newbuild, high-debt, subsidised housing is added to 'top up' this part of the stock.

Seen in a broader rental systemic perspective in terms of maturation, the historical dynamic would appear to be as follows. After a long period during the middle years of the post-war period when rent regulated newbuild accounted for between two-thirds and 95 per cent of total rental newbuild the proportion of first-tier rent regulated housing had risen to over 30 per cent in 1968. As already indicated, this proportion may have already fallen to 26 per cent by 1987. The proportion of rent regulated dwellings fell from a peak of 41 per cent of all rental newbuild in the period 1958 to 1968 to 22 per cent in 1969 to 1978, and to 8 per cent in 1979 to 1987.

So with on average a maximum of 25 years of rent regulation it can be seen that the proportion of rent regulated housing will continue to fall. The decline will be dampened somewhat as a result of a recent increase in rent regulated newbuild, but the trend will in any event continue downward for some time in the future.

The German system can therefore be characterised as a part-profit unitary rental market, the unitary character of which is attained not by harmonisation but by a fragmentation and diversification of landlordism that is further complicated by the changing status of landlordism with respect to subsidies and rent regulation over time. The result is a rental market of kaleidoscopic variety and complexity but undoubtedly with a significant element of cost rent market influence that changes over time.

The long-term direction of development of such a market can only be speculated. The conventional anglo-saxon wisdom is that the current decline in the proportion of cost rental housing is part of the international residualisation process of the rental sector. However, it may well be that the current downward trend in cost rental newbuild will result in a lessening of the rent-dampening effect. This in turn will, on the one hand mature the cost rental stock thereby countering to some extent the smaller size of the stock in its market impact, and on the other hand stimulate a new expansion in cost rental newbuild, thereby initiating a new rent-dampening phase in the cycle of the rental market's development.

Such a market may well exhibit, therefore, a self-adjusting dynamic between cost and profit rental housing. As the proportion of cost rental housing rises cost rental housing begins to exert a more powerful downward pull on rents in general. As a result of this, rents in the market as a whole fall thereby increasing demand for profit rental housing at the expense of cost rental housing. As cost rental newbuild declines in response to this shift in demand, private rents gradually float upwards, despite the dampening effect of an ageing stock of cost rental housing. When rents are high once more, there is renewed demand for cost rental newbuild, which results in the cycle being renewed. Indeed, it is possible that the current increase in cost rental newbuild in Germany is the start of a reaction to rapidly rising rents during the 1980s which in turn is largely the result of the declining share of cost rental housing on the rental market.

SWITZERLAND

Switzerland has the highest proportion of rental housing in Western Europe, comprising nearly 70 per cent of its total housing stock. Of this, only a very small proportion – some 4 per cent – is public rental housing. Access to public rental housing is stringently means tested, production is limited to the minimum needed to house the poorest sections of the population, and special subsidies are provided to bring rents down to a level which its tenants can afford.

The private rental market consists of a number of different categories of landlord. In 1980 63 per cent of dwellings were rental apartments, and a further 4 per cent co-operative apartments which involve tenant capital investment that is closely regulated (Federal Statistics office 1980 Census, quoted in Gurtner, 1988, p. 361). Another classification from the same source (Gurtner, 1988, p. 362) gives 65.5 per cent of occupied dwellings owned by individuals, 16.5 per cent owned by legal entities, with a further 15 per cent owned by construction and property companies, including investment funds.

These categories make it difficult to judge the percentage of the stock that is owned by cost rental organisations. Switzerland's strict secrecy laws concerning all aspects of finance, including property ownership and asset values mean that social scientists have to rely on crude estimates for their data. It may be, for example, that a considerable proportion of the 'legal entities' and even some of the property companies are in fact non-profit organisations of various kinds. However, it is probably safest to assume for the purposes of this discussion that the percentage of cost rental housing is so modest that it is not sufficient to have a major impact in dampening rents.

On the surface, therefore, the Swiss rental system bears many of the hallmarks of a dualist one. The small Swiss public rental sector would appear to have many similarities to the command systems of public renting in English-speaking countries. However, there are major differences. In the first place, public rental housing is indistinguishable from other forms of rental housing since it is subjected to the same construction standards. No attempt has been made to ghettoise public renting as part of a wider strategy to make it less attractive. Second, and much more important, private rental housing is also both subsidised and rent regulated, though in a different manner from that employed in dualist systems.

The system operates at two separate levels of subsidy. The first level is common to all rental housing providers since there are provision subsidies made available to all landlords in return for which they agree to abide by the rent regulations and minimum construction and equipment standards. In this, it has considerable similarities with the Swedish and German systems. Over and above this are subsidies to bring rental housing within reach of the poor. Although public rental housing tends to be the main recipient of these subsidies, all landlords may apply for them and so the percentage of new construction built as low-income housing varies from year to year, in recent years rising to around 20 per cent of new production.

Dwellings built or renovated with federal loans at subsidised rates of interest are subject to rent control for the first ten years. After this there is no rent regulation as such but tenants have the right to have their rent reviewed and there are a number of criteria used in judging such cases. The two most important of these is that rents must reflect original construction costs plus a modest margin for profit and that rents must be roughly in line with the average level of rents in the area.

These two criteria combine to produce rents that are rather similar to the way in which Swedish use-value rents were originally conceived. That is, they are cost rents which are modified by comparative factors. The local comparative rent element has similarities with the German *Mietspiegel*.

This rent-setting system allows the preponderance of older dwellings with lower costs to lead the market, rather than the market being led by newbuild prices as is the case in an unregulated market. But at the same time it encourages cross pooling by landlords to bring newbuild rents down.

The Swiss system therefore has a substantial element of cost-based use-value rent setting. This is evidenced in that in 1986 a low proportion – approximately 20 per cent – of household income was spent on rent. The system is also a unitary one in that all rental housing irrespective of ownership is both eligible for public subsidy and liable to follow the rent regulations.

Where the Swiss system seems to differ from Sweden, The Netherlands and Germany is that, as far as Swiss statistics allow us to conclude, cost rental housing seems to play a marginal role or at least does not play a market leadership role, nor have a market-dampening effect. The system relies entirely on a two-tier rent regulation system similar to that in Germany – a temporary newbuild subsidy and a cost-based mirror rent. However, this conclusion must be qualified until such time as further information can be obtained on the ownership structure of the housing stock.

Part III

Research and policy implications

Introduction

This final part considers some of the research and policy dimensions of the model developed in Part I and exemplified in Part II. Part III therefore explores some of the issues that need to be tackled in order to develop research and policy analysis further.

Chapter 9 examines the dynamics of unitary rental markets. Three related issues are dealt with here. The first is the development of a simple classification of unitary rental markets. This is derived from the varieties of policy strategies that were revealed in the case studies discussed in the preceding chapter.

The classification is based on the manner in which the relationship between profit and non-profit forms of rental provision is structured. It is the balance between these forms of rental provision that, in all the countries examined with the possible exception of Switzerland, determines the extent to which rents, standards of housing, and security of tenure will be more in line with cost-covering as against profit-making principles. The key dimension here is the extent to which cost rental housing is able to impact on the market behaviour of profit-orientated landlords.

Following on from this, I examine the type of unitary rental market that is most interesting analytically. This is the unitary rental market in which cost and profit forms of provision compete with one another. Competition between cost and profit renting constitutes the central feature of all unitary rental markets at least during the initial period of transition from dualism, and often throughout and beyond the transition. Indeeed, it is largely this that distinguishes such a market from dualist systems. The dynamics of this competition, and the role of maturation in it, make the study of unitary rental markets particularly interesting, and provide researchers with a fertile subject for the development of new kinds of analyses.

Finally, in the light of the preceding discussion I return to the matter of the Romeo error made in comparative rental housing research. The aim here is to show how symptoms in unitary rental markets are only superficially similar to those in dualist systems. This superficial similarity has lulled researchers into believing that their analyses of dualist systems apply also to unitary rental markets. In fact, the frame of analysis that is needed in order to understand how unitary rental markets operate is quite different from the traditional perspective from which dualist rental markets have been analysed hitherto.

Chapter 10 examines in a very rudimentary manner some of the implications of implementing a shift in policy strategy from a dualist system to a unitary rental market. The long-term nature of policy strategies limits this discussion to a general level. The main concern is to indicate the principal areas of housing policy that would need to be realigned over a number of years in order to accomplish such a shift.

The discussion begins with a summary of some of the main arguments in favour of such a shift in policy strategy. It is something of a paradox that at a time when the return to the market has such wide political support there is still no real opposition to – let alone hubris over – the public rental command economy that is such an integral part of the housing systems of many industrialised societies. This makes it necessary to present the case for such a change in policy strategy.

The key to entering the transition from dualism to a unitary market lies in restructuring the public rental sector to enable the housing organisations to attain autonomy from political decision making. Much of the discussion therefore focuses upon this and the kinds of market strategies that the new cost rent housing organisations will need to adopt in order to compete with profit renting. This includes, crucially, rent setting.

However, it will also be necessary to restructure the housing allowance and social security systems. This in turn points to the fact that housing is ultimately inextricable from wider policy issues. This is particularly so when attempting to change policy strategy.

Even more intriguing, it unavoidably involves confronting issues of principle concerning the structuring of the welfare state. This is almost completely uncharted territory for policy researchers, and raises important issues for the conduct of future comparative welfare research and is the subject of Chapter 11.

9 Unitary rental markets: towards a systematisation

A TYPOLOGY OF UNITARY RENTAL MARKETS

Cost renting as 'dominant', 'leading' or 'influencing'

The above descriptions of the rental systems of a number of countries are, with the exception of Sweden, sketchy and preliminary. There is very little data on the workings of unitary rental markets. This is mainly because, as we have seen, the concept is new and so the empirical data that has been collected has not addressed the specific issues that such a system throws up. As a result, little or no research has been done on them. Most importantly, because housing researchers have used an anglo-saxon paradigm they have in general failed to ask the right questions and so not collected the relevant data. In this sense, the comparative rental housing literature is a classic case of a conservative dominant paradigm that selects which facts are of interest and then produces findings which confirm the validity of the paradigm. A few general observations can be made, however.

Each of the countries considered in the preceding section – as well as Denmark and Austria, and possibly additional countries about which we still know insufficient to make a judgement – has taken its own route to the establishment of a unitary rental market. They all have in common the fact that they seek to minimise the differences between various forms of rental provision and they are all based to varying degrees and in different ways on developing a demand-sensitive rental market based partially or entirely on cost-related rents.

Sweden, The Netherlands and Germany have all encouraged the development of a cost rental sector which has been first built up in size and then private profit-orientated renting has been increasingly exposed to direct competition from cost renting. It is less clear whether this has also applied in Switzerland, which must be treated as a somewhat different case in the absence of more adequate information. Concerning the first three countries, we may roughly distinguish between the extent to which cost rental housing determines overall rent levels: that is, whether cost rental housing dominates the rental market, leads it, or influences it.

The Netherlands has a rental market in which the overwhelming majority of housing is cost rental. Privately owned profit-orientated rental housing comprises such a small proportion of the total housing stock that market rents are almost entirely determined by the cost structures of an increasingly mature cost rental housing stock. Cost rental housing therefore *dominates* the rental market. For this reason, too, there is no harmonisation problematic to contend with. In spite of this however, The Netherlands has not yet made the transition from rent regulation to free market rents, though deregulation is presaged by the withdrawal of state funding for the construction of new rental housing.

In Sweden, where half the rental stock is owned by cost rental housing companies, a shift towards demand-sensitive rents is well under way, and here cost rental housing acts as market leader for profit-orientated private rents. It therefore *leads* the rental market.

However, as we have noted, Sweden is at present undergoing a transition to freer rent setting and so it is not yet clear whether cost renting will continue to lead the market or whether some sort of unregulated system will emerge in which cost rental housing will lose its leadership role and develop into one where they act in the more limited capacity of constituting a braking influence on private rents. This would constitute a shift from a leading to an influencing role for Swedish cost rental housing.

The German and Swiss systems are ones in which cost rental housing *influences* private rents by dampening them to a greater or lesser degree. This is more apparent in Germany where cost rental housing, reinforced by subsidised (and therefore rent regulated) private rental housing, comprises a substantial proportion of the total housing stock.

However, in both Germany and Switzerland there remains a substantial element of rent regulation based primarily on making the granting of subsidised rental housing loans subject to the acceptance of some kind of cost-covering rent-setting system. Over and above this, both countries define a reasonable rent as one which has a strong comparable element in it and that is principally formed in such a way as to prevent rents rising to the level at which tenants receive no imputed rent at all.

The transition from rent regulation to completely relying on cost rents as a means of dampening private rents is as yet only in its early stages in Germany and Switzerland. The crucial two variables determining when completing the transition is possible will be the relative size of the cost rental sector and its level of maturity. It is important to bear in mind that we are dealing here with very long-term processes. The cost rental stocks of all European countries – with the partial exception of Britain – are all relatively immature. They have expanded rapidly until the mid-1970s and their coverage of the market is still far from complete. In particular, the rental markets of inner-city areas are often still only weakly influenced by cost rental housing organisations.

'Cost' versus 'part-profit' unitary rental markets

The three types of rental market – 'dominated', 'led', and 'influenced' by cost rental housing – produce two different kinds of unitary rental markets. The first is produced when markets are dominated by cost rental housing. Here no harmonisation problematic exists as profit-orientated renting either does not exist or is too minor to have a significant impact on rents. The second is produced when markets are either led or influenced by cost rental housing, and here harmonisation results in synergy with profit-orientated renting which has its own dynamic.

Cost unitary rental markets

In markets dominated by cost renting, profit renting plays a marginal role, if any at all. Cost rental housing organisations therefore need react only to household demand. Demand will express itself in a high vacancy rate for overpriced housing and in long queues and possibly a black market in key money for attractive dwellings. The former is a chronic aspect of command economy public renting which manifests in the phenomenon of 'hard-to-let' estates. The black market is less common in anglo-saxon command economies since bureaucratic control of the allocations process is normally extremely tight.

Both these phenomena are essentially uneconomical consequences of faulty price setting. They are just as damaging to a non-profit economy as a profit-orientated one. High vacancy rates result in lost income, which in turn places the burden of the vacant properties onto the shoulders of all the tenants. A black market that results from underpricing means that the lost rent is pocketed privately by outgoing tenants instead of contributing to the rent pool.

In a command economy inefficiencies are an acceptable price for the state to pay for a residualised public rental sector. It is also a function of the existence of a subsistence-level social security system that is insensitive to rent differentials. This point will be returned to in Chapter 10 when we consider what changes would be needed to a command system to convert it to a market system. Here it need only be noted that an undifferentiated rent rebate and social security system does not encourage public rental housing agencies to reduce the rents of hard-to-let estates. In a sense, market inefficiencies are an acceptable political and economic price to pay for being able to sustain a command economy public rental sector and a subsistence-level social security system. In a market economy such gross inefficiency is unacceptable since tenants are seen as customers and not welfare dependents.

Rents can be made demand-sensitive by the simple expedient of demand-sensitive rent pooling. This enables less attractive housing to be let at rents well below costs because it is cross-subsidised by the higher rents of more attractive cheaper housing. That is, a market effect is created by widening the differentials between the rents of high and low demand housing. In a system where social security incomes are graduated in relation to rents this makes both demand and supply income sensitive. The net rental income is still cost covering for the stock as a whole, so that the non-profit principle is adhered to.

The more mature the housing stock is the more cross pooling can be employed and the larger the rent differentials can be between high and low demand housing. The wider the rent differentials can be made through cross pooling the more demand can be evened out between attractive and less attractive housing. Such a system results in a cost rental market in which the pooled rents of the stock exactly cover the total real costs of the stock even though large variations may exist in rents within the stock.

Part-profit unitary rental markets

By contrast, rental markets in which cost rents lead or influence private profit-orientated rents will result in a rental market in which profit-orientated rents are dampened to a greater or lesser degree. In such a market, private landlords can normally extract higher than cost-covering rents. Just how much will depend on how strong and competitive a market position cost rental housing has. The dampening effect of cost rents on private rents will therefore result in a part-profit rental market.

The degree of profit extraction in such a market will vary over time and will often be unevenly spread across the housing stock. It will normally be the case that the older and often more mature profit rental stock will be concentrated in the inner urban areas and here the influence on rents of the less well represented cost rental housing will be weaker than in areas where cost rental housing represents a larger proportion of the stock. This has commonly been the case in the majority of countries over most of the post-war period.

The extent of profit-making will vary considerably due to a number of factors. The larger and more diverse the cost rental stock is and the more mature it is the more competition it will be able to offer to profit renting. This in turn will mean that profits can be more heavily dampened.

Let us consider a little further the dynamic behind the operation of a part-profit rental market. In theory, the ability of profit-orientated landlords to make profits over and above cost-covering levels could mean that the supply of new private rental housing increases. However, in a unitary rental market the level of profit extraction is crucially determined by the relative levels of maturation in the private and cost rental housing stocks. As already indicated, the more mature cost rental housing is, the greater will be its dampening effect on profit-orientated rents. Therefore, any increase in the supply of profit renting that results from increased profitability adds to the front loading of profit rental housing, slowing down the maturation process and thereby dampening profits.

Maturation and profit extraction therefore must be understood as countervailing forces. The more mature the profit rental stock is the more profits can be extracted. As front loading decreases so profitability rises. As profitability rises this stimulates landlords to increase newbuild. But this decelerates the process of maturation, shrinking profits and reducing newbuild. As front loading decreases so profitability rises and the cycle is begun again.

This observation needs to be somewhat qualified by the fact that at least some increase in profit-orientated housing supply may come from conversions of owner occupied properties into rental properties to take advantage of high rents. Such conversions will increase the size of the rental sector at the expense of the owner occupied sector but will not add to the rental sector's front loading. However, the extent to which such conversions of existing housing takes place is likely to be greater in societies where the owner occupied market is large and where security of tenure is low. This state of affairs is most common in 'home-owning' societies with dualist rental systems.

But what happens if profit-orientated landlords, despite being able to make substantial profits, do not sustain a level of new construction comparable to that of cost rental housing organisations? Clearly, the rapid maturation of the profit rental stock that this would result in would increase the relative maturity of private to cost renting, and to that extent would increase still further private profits. However, it would also mean that as a result of lack of profit-orientated newbuild and continued cost rental newbuild the relative size of the private rental housing stock would decline. This in turn would further increase the influence of cost rents on the rental market, and possibly in the long run lead to the creation of a rental market dominated by cost rental housing.

THE DYNAMICS OF UNITARY RENTAL MARKETS

The short and medium term result of a rapidly maturing profit rental sector will be an increase in landlord profit extraction and a corresponding decline in imputed rental income for private tenants. However, the end result would be a growing cost rental sector. This would either strongly dampen private rents or would result in the elimination of private profit-orientated renting and the emergence of a unitary cost rental market of the sort that exists in The Netherlands.

This latter scenario is, in fact, quite likely. The historical evidence, and what we know of the investment record of private landlords from economic theory clearly suggests this. Private investment in housing has always been highly unreliable and variable. This is not just because of the varying profitability of the rental market itself. It is more crucially due to the considerable fluctuations in the relative profitability of rental housing investment as against other kinds of investment.

Thus, for example, the outbreak of the Second World War led to a substantial increase in the relative profitability of war industries and this resulted in a massive flight of capital from housing, even though the profitability of housing remained largely unchanged. Indeed, it was precisely this phenomenon which provided the stimulus in many countries for the setting up of cost rental housing organisations in the first place.

Is a unitary part-profit rental market then merely a transitional stage on the way to the development of a unitary cost rental market? The economic dynamic of maturation would clearly suggest that this is so. Cost rental housing organisations can always undercut private profit rental housing, given similar levels of maturity of their respective housing stocks. There may well be, therefore, a built-in long-run tendency for cost renting to squeeze profit renting out of rental markets.

However, such a judgement may be premature, for two reasons. The first is that cost rental stocks in most countries are only now starting to attain levels of maturity and numbers of dwellings that give them the market power to seriously undercut private rental housing. It may therefore be several decades before any large-scale decline in private rental housing's share of unitary rental markets is evident (The Netherlands is clearly an exception here). And in any case, it is still very rare for cost rental housing to be well represented in older inner-city areas.

So at least for the foreseeable future, there will be key urban areas where cost renting has relatively weak market influence. However, these are lesser reasons. For example, it is always possible for cost rental housing organisations to begin to invest in older inner-city dwellings at the expense of greensite newbuild, buying them up on a large enough scale to enable them to ultimately influence rents. Such a strategy would, initially at least, create an immature inner-city cost rental stock and would therefore not affect profits for some time. But it would be a perfectly rational long-term development strategy.

The second reason is more pertinent. The scenario of the transition from part-profit to cost rental market assumes that government policy strategies remain unchanged. Yet, as we have seen, government policy as an expression of a wider strategic approach to the rental market is a crucial variable in determining the role of cost rental housing on the rental market. It may well be, therefore, that there will be strong political pressure to prevent the eclipse of profit renting either by propping it up in some way or by placing restrictions on cost rental housing in order to keep private profits up.

The transition from a part-profit to a cost rental system may therefore be thwarted by policies to maintain the status quo or even to abandon the unitary market altogether. In the latter case, a dualist system would be reinstated by increasingly placing cost renting under a command economy to shelter private profit renting from market competition. And given the persuasive impact of the anglo-saxon model, such an outcome is not at all impossible.

Such a situation would therefore represent a historic juncture that took place in a country with a unitary rental market rather than a dualist one, and at a relatively late stage in the maturation process. The aim in such circumstances would not be to prevent the emergence of a large cost rental housing market by sustaining dualism but to prevent a part-profit rental market from developing into a cost rental market. It does not appear that this particular kind of historic juncture has ever emerged in a country moving towards a unitary rental market – at least not yet.

There is therefore no automatic development of a cost rental market out of a part-profit one. This underlines the fact that the influence of the state is decisive in determining what form the rental market will take. Instead there are a variety of sharply contrasting rental market policy strategies – dualist, unitary part-profit and unitary cost rental – together with the different ways in which unitary part-profit rental markets can be, and are, organised in a number of industrialised European countries.

UNITARY RENTAL MARKET DYNAMICS AND THE ROMEO ERROR

In Chapter 2, I suggested that, as a result of ethnocentricity, comparative rental research has fallen into the Romeo error – deriving a pessimistic prognosis from misinterpreting superficially similar symptoms. We have noted that a common observation in comparative rental research is a tendency for rental housing in general and public or cost rental housing in particular to become increasingly residualised. A rising rate of owner occupation and tendencies towards increasing concentrations of low-income earners and social security recipients in public or cost renting can be identified in many, if not most, countries including at least some of those with unitary rental markets. Power (1993) shows this for the two countries with unitary rental markets, Germany and Denmark, that she has examined.

In a dualist system the residualisation of public renting is often a matter of deliberate policy. When this is the case, as few as possible middle-income earners are desired in public renting, and the aim is to 'target' public renting to those households who are in the most desperate housing need, and, moreover, to as small a proportion of these as can be contrived. The more households that can be forced out into the profit markets of owner occupation and private renting the better.

In a social rental market there is, of course, no similar attempt to politically steer cost renting towards providing housing exclusively or even principally for those most in need. On the contrary, the aim is to prevent the emergence of a low-income housing sector. However, because renting in a unitary market is the obvious choice of housing for low-income earners it will nevertheless be the case that the poorest households are found disproportionately in the rental sector and often in cost rental housing.

This, however, merely reinforces the impression that 'policy does not matter' and that similar common, yet unspecified, deep underlying structural processes are at work. It is not possible to pin down housing researchers on this point due to the essentially empirical nature of the argument. However, the innuendo is clearly that owning is inherently more attractive than renting.

Behind this innuendo lies the common-sense explanation that as standards of living rise, more people can afford to become owner occupiers. Implicit in this assumption is that most people naturally prefer to buy than to rent and that as soon as they can do so they will. According to this argument, then, the trend towards owner occupation will be universal and independent of the type of rental system a country has.

The question that now needs to be asked is that given the existence of two contrasting rental systems, are there different processes at work in societies with unitary rental markets that could explain the trend to owner occupation in terms of a different logic from that in societies with dualist rental systems? I wish to argue that this is indeed the case. The integration of cost and profit rental housing into a unitary rental market is a long-term strategy that, because of the nature of the process of maturation, takes many decades to achieve. The strategy is essentially post-war in origin, and so far in no society has the policy strategy succeeded in creating a mature, fully harmonised unitary rental market where the cost rental stock covers the full range of dwelling types and locations. Different aspects of this may be considered in turn.

Immaturity

The first point to note, then, is that all the countries with unitary rental market policies that have been discussed above still possess cost rental stocks that have a significant degree of immaturity. They have all been undergoing a sustained period of expansion necessary to create such a stock virtually from scratch. Indeed, it is only in the last decade or so that this rapid expansion and the heavy front loading that it entails has declined significantly.

To this it might be added that there has been a widespread reliance on loans with an amortisation of half a century or more, in contrast to loans of twenty-five years or so in owner occupation. This means that very little cost rental housing is entirely debt free. Much of the little that has recently become debt free has been re-mortgaged to pay for modernisation.

Long-term mortgages and loans of this sort have the effect of re-distributing the cost of housing from new to old. This has the added disadvantage of reducing the scope for demand-sensitive rent pooling to create a differentiated rent structure that reflects demand accurately. So in addition to the continuing – if falling – high levels of immaturity of much of the cost rental stock the use of long-term loans further limits the implementation of demand-sensitive cost-covering rent setting.

Besides the question of maturity, there are several further factors to consider.

Market 'patchiness' in part-profit markets

The availability of cost rental housing remains geographically restricted. It is most commonly available in the middle and outer sub-urbs of urban areas. Inner-city rental housing remains predominantly in the ownership of profit-orientated landlords.

Here we must distinguish between different types of unitary rental markets. Where cost renting dominates or leads, the ownership of the inner-city housing stock is of relatively minor importance, since profit rents will be kept relatively low. It is in societies where cost renting influences, rather than dominates or leads, the profit sector that there will often be a weak impact on profit renting in parts of the market where cost renting is still under-represented.

The choice of cost rental housing in terms of its geographical location and urban milieu therefore remains limited in a part-profit unitary rental market in which cost renting influences profit rent levels. This, again, is a limitation that can be overcome in the long run, as cost renting begins to expand in inner-urban areas, although it will take many decades to achieve.

Dwelling-type specialisation

The availability of cost rental housing in a wide range of dwelling types remains restricted. The emphasis has been on providing flatted apartment blocks, and relatively little cost rental detached and semi-detached housing has been produced. Much of the demand for owner occupation can therefore not be separated out from the demand for detached and semi-detached housing.

The historical prioritising of flats over houses must be understood as a necessary concomitant of the initial expansion of cost renting to meet the huge shortfall of housing that has existed during the early post-war decades. A diversification of the stock through an expansion in the production or acquisition of cost rental houses would be a natural future development by any enterprising cost rental organisation, and may well be one of the changes to take place in the coming decades. Meanwhile, some of the unsatisfied demand for cheap rental houses will be diverted into the owner occupied sector.

The harmonisation transition

As we have seen, unitary rental markets are still passing through a long transition from dualist to unitary market organisation. The harmonisation problematic results in some sacrifice of market adaptability of rents to prevent profit rents from rising to unacceptably high levels and thereby undermining security of tenure in a large part of the stock. Rent regulation in profit renting remains an important dimension of unitary rental market organisation, although, as we have seen, there is a general trend towards the phasing out of rent regulation in many countries.

Rent regulation necessarily has a distorting market impact by increasing demand for rent regulated housing. This demand cannot be satisfied, and so a part of it will be diverted into other forms of housing. Rent regulation is therefore bound to impact on tenure preferences in a way that encourages a shift to owner occupation.

Similar trends, different processes

My argument is therefore that in unitary rental countries where there is a trend towards rising rates of owner occupation and an increase in the proportion of low-income earners in renting this must be seen as the result of a specific dynamic. The short- and even the medium-term trends may be similar to that found in dualist rental systems but the causes are different.

This is not to deny that as standards of living have risen during the post-war period and as housing shortages have been overcome there is a tendency for owner occupation to increase, particularly among higher- and middle-income earners. By the same token, rising living standards have extended the possibility of more lower-income households both being formed earlier and at all, and capable of demanding higher space and privacy standards. A falling proportion of high-income earners and a rising proportion of low-income earners in social renting is therefore understandable irrespective of what rental system is created, but only to a certain extent. Some of the trend to owner occupation may well be a product of rental market structuring. It is therefore important to be clear about the differing nature of that trend in dualist and unitary systems.

In dualist systems we are witnessing processes of extreme residualisation of renting, in which rates of owner occupation are approaching 70 per cent of households, and the public rental sectors of which contain very high concentrations of disadvantaged households. In the South Australian Housing Trust, for example, we noted that rent rebates were received by 70 per cent of tenants.

In unitary rental markets, by contrast, there are quite different levels of such phenomena. These countries have rental markets that account for between 40 and 70 per cent of the total housing stock. Increases in owner occupation and the proportion of higher-income earners in renting start off from vastly different base levels.

There are, unfortunately, difficulties in collecting long-term trend data on the social composition of tenures that allow international comparisons that hold constant both the relative size of the rental market and its structure. Because of this, housing researchers, noting a similar trend and not recognising the qualitative difference between unitary and dualist rental systems, draw upon their knowledge of how dualist rental systems operate and fail to distinguish between the different dynamics that are involved. They jump to the conclusion that they are witnessing similar long-term processes. They thereby commit the Romeo error when they explain the superficially similar trends as being caused by the same underlying processes.

An alternative explanation

Unitary rental markets must be seen as undergoing a long drawn-out transition phase, during which an attractive rental market is being slowly formed. In this process the rental system is being restructured in such a way as to maximise its attractiveness to households. We may therefore judge the success of this policy strategy by the rate of household loss to owner occupation and the rate of marginalisation of renting relative to societies with dualist systems and taking into account changes in the size of the rental market, the proportion that is cost rental and how mature the cost rental stock is, rather than its absolute existence or otherwise.

Equally important, we have seen that unitary rental strategies vary widely and resulting rental markets have contrasting structures. The marginalisation phenomenon will therefore take different forms and will occur to different degrees and at different rates, or possibly will not take place at all. We may therefore expect that there will be no uniform tendency towards marginalisation in unitary rental markets.

Additionally, we need to take into acount the cyclical nature of the maturation process and its impact on the demand and supply of cost rental housing in part-profit unitary rental markets. Over and above the long-term process of transition from dualism to a unitary market, there may be in such markets cycles of rising and falling demand for cost renting as periods of heavy and light front loading succeed one another and as the maturation process changes tempo.

Finally, we need to be aware that the transition to unitary markets is not an inevitable and politically conflict-free process. The 1980s in particular have been a period when anglo-saxon neo-liberalism has put unitary rental policy strategy on the defensive in several countries. The harmonisation problematic can lead to policy strategy changes that either speed up the transition to a unitary rental market or subvert it by weakening the cost rental sector or even by reintroducing dualism. Some of the trend towards marginalisation in unitary markets may therefore be the product of ideological assaults on it from the supporters of dualism. This leads us to examine rental policy strategies as implicit agendas.

RENTAL POLICY STRATEGIES AS IMPLICIT AGENDAS

The entrenchment of policy strategies

I have argued that major turning points in policy strategy towards the rental sector – what I term historic junctures – are the product of a temporal concurrence of the emergence of a major difference in rent levels between cost and profit renting and the emergence of a distinct policy strategy towards the rental sector. The result is a rent-differential crisis which forms the policy rationale for entrenching a particular kind of policy strategy.

This concurrence is not, of course, a purely random event. Often the emergence of a new – or much more clearly formulated and often more radical – policy strategy towards the rental sector has been stimulated by growing rent differentials. But even when this is the case, there is usually an existing predisposition towards a given rent policy strategy that has fairly broad implicit support in society.

The process whereby a policy strategy emerges now requires some consideration. A policy strategy is given practical expression in numerous major and minor policy decisions over time. As measures succeed one another and accumulate over time, a policy strategy becomes increasingly entrenched. This will often happen without explicit formulation or clear goals. It may even never be recognised as a policy strategy, nor be so clearly identified that it can easily be challengeable with an alternative policy strategy.

A policy strategy is therefore often very intangible and unapparent as a set of principles that can be used as guidelines for policy making. It may be so deeply rooted in the practical day to day decision-making routines of government that it lacks conscious form. It will then simply be part of the taken-for-granted assumptions of local and national politicians, administrators and policy makers.

British policy strategy is a particularly extreme example that has developed slowly over many decades and reached its full flowering during the 1980s. There has always been considerable political consensus in Britain that public renting should constitute a separate dual rental sector parallel and unintegrated with private renting. Even the supporters of council housing have defended the status quo rather than attempt to argue offensively for a distinctive and radical cost rental market role for public renting.

It is therefore only the juncture between a delayed rent-differential crisis and a period of particularly intense conservative reaction that makes the British historic juncture of the early 1980s so dramatic in appearance. And given the absence of a policy strategy alternative or even any critical analysis of the dominant policy strategy, the paradox of instituting an ever more centralised command economy in council housing while paying lip service to 'the market' has gone unchallenged.

In other countries where a dualist system has been developed, such as Australia and New Zealand, consensus has also been high over the need for strong centralised state control over public renting and the development of a monotenural housing system dominated by owner occupation by hampering free market competition. However, with the partial exception of New Zealand (Davidson, 1992), these countries never developed a large public rental sector in the first place as had happened in Britain. The reaction against the growing competitiveness of public renting has therefore not been as strong as it has been in Britain. The rent-differential crisis in Australia in the mid-1970s was therefore not as traumatic as in Britain, while a similar reaction in New Zealand that took place in the early 1950s and again in more recent years has been likewise much less dramatic.

It would be particularly interesting to examine a country going through a rent-differential crisis where the hegemonic position of the dualist policy strategy is less strongly entrenched than it is in English-speaking countries and where alternative policy strategies – particularly that of the market-based unitary rental system – are explicated and debated and therefore constitute an alternative model from which the command economy approach to public renting can be challenged.

The hegemonic position of such market-based unitary rental strategies in countries like Sweden, The Netherlands, Germany and Switzerland is much less strongly entrenched than the command economy model is in English-speaking countries. We need to bear in mind that the concept of the social market economy has always been seen as a third way that lies between the two extremes of the profit-driven market and the command economy. It therefore lends itself less easily to the sort of rhetorical hyperbole that has been a feature of both these extreme forms from time to time.

However, social market rental policy strategy is by no means under ideological siege and in some countries is well entrenched. The Netherlands has already almost attained a full unitary cost rental market, without, it would seem, any major debate or controversy over the adoption of this path. In Austria – or at least in Vienna which accounts for a third of all Austrian housing – Matznetter (1992) argues that the major vested interests in housing combine to sustain a system that is rapidly moving towards what I am describing here as a Dutch-type unitary cost rental market. The corporatist system of balancing different religious and other interests – which also operates in Dutch housing – would seem to be sustaining, probably as a side-effect and unintentionally, a unitary rental market hegemonic ideology.

For Germany and Sweden, however, the unitary rental market approach is under periodic challenge from the proponents of dualism: a challenge that varies in its intensity both between the countries and in each country over time. The challenge is probably stronger in Sweden than in Germany, because Sweden has relied entirely on state provision of cost rental housing, even though mediated by arms-length cost rental housing companies, and because the harmonisation problematic is harder to resolve in the market leadership model that Sweden has adopted. In Germany, the complex and shifting nature of the unitary rental market in terms of types of provision and types of subsidisation that change over time make it much less easy to 'unscramble' the unitary rental market by identifying a scapegoat public rental sector against which ideological venom may be directed and that can be targeted for segregation and asset stripping in order to create a dualist system.

That the unitary rental systems in Sweden and Germany are both challengeable is partly because the unitary rental market is the product of a corporatist-based political compromise between competing housing interests. The resulting consensus is therefore more fragile and kept implicit so as not to disturb the balance. Alternating political party triumphalism and ideological polarisation of the sort that takes place in Britain are inappropriate in such a system. In addition, the conservative reaction of the 1980s has been an international movement originating in and backed by ideologically informed English language academic debate by theorists such as Hayek and Friedmann.

Ideological assaults on unitary strategy

The conservative argument against unitary rental markets in societies which have such a rental market is two-pronged. The first of these exploits the necessarily very long running harmonisation problematic that derives from the essentially transitional nature of rent control in unitary rental housing markets. We have noted that harmonisation is a major problem in moving towards a unitary rental market and that rent controls are only gradually being withdrawn as the cost rental housing stock matures in order that cost rents should continue to influence or if possible determine overall rent levels.

The opponents of a free unitary rental market argue for an immediate lifting of all rent controls to foreshorten such a phasing in. The result of this would be to drive rents up to enable profit-orientated landlords to maximise profits and to encourage as many tenants as possible to switch to owner occupation. This is made possible because there is no recognition or acknowledgement of the existence of a 'harmonisation problematic'. Rent regulation is defined instead as heavy-handed state control that should be abolished.

The second prong of the ideological attack on the unitary rental market (or its potential) is based on the need to greatly weaken the market position of cost rental organisations and to residualise them. A large cost rental sector allowed to compete on the open market for tenants will always have a great advantage over profit-orientated landlords and will constantly exert downward pressure on rents. The very existence of a cost rental housing sector – whether co-operative, private housing trust, local government or state owned is therefore a key target of those who wish to shelter profit landlordism from cost rental competition.

To undermine the market strength of cost rental housing organisations, the opponents of a unitary rental market argue for the compulsory sale of cost rental housing to tenants at extreme sub-market prices, and/or for the conversion of cost rental housing organisations into profit-orientated companies. This is normally proposed either by compulsory sales to private landlords as is being attempted in Britain, or by simply converting cost rental organisations into profit-orientated housing. This latter can be achieved in a number of different ways, for example by the state clawing back surpluses made by forcing cost rental housing to charge market rents – as is happening in Britain and Australia – or by the simple expedient of 'privatisation' by selling cost rental housing organisations on the stock exchange, as is argued should be done in Sweden (Meyerson *et al.*, 1990, pp. 142–3).

But no matter which strategy is adopted – whether it is converting cost renting into tenant ownership and individual owner occupation or whether it is converting cost renting into private profit renting or some combination of both, the goal is the same. It is to shelter profit-orientated renting and – indirectly, and more importantly – owner occupation from competition by ensuring that the central state takes measures to undermine cost rental organisations.

The more fragile hegemonic position of the unitary rental market strategy is therefore due to a combination of the long transition time needed to attain a fully functioning market and the existence of an alternative strategy which attempts to depict the command economy of public renting in the dualist rental system of English-speaking countries as the genuine representative of free market competition between renting and owning. The periodic maturation crises of the command economy are as difficult in their own way to deal with as the harmonisation problematic of the unitary rental market. But without a clear understanding of the dynamics involved and, more important, without any alternative model to propose, they remain ideologically unchallenged and can be represented as manifesting a 'natural' distaste for 'unmarket-like' state involvement in rental housing.

It is this that makes arguments, however well meaning, by housing researchers that the residualisation of cost renting is an inevitable international trend, so invidious. Such arguments reinforce, sometimes unwittingly, the dominance of the anglo-saxon model by trivialising the alternative models as mere 'variations' without wider theoretical and conceptual significance. The process of residualisation is depicted as ineluctable and as structural and therefore apolitical and essentially non-ideological.

The implication of such analysis is that deeper structural processes are at work – processes that are left only vaguely hinted at – and that public policy or ideological conflict play no role at all, or at best only a marginal, secondary role. And this in turn undermines and counters any attempt to develop an alternative paradigm that might be used to challenge dominant command economy dualist rental models.

THE ANGLO-SAXON HEGEMONY AND EASTERN EUROPE

The collapse of communism in Eastern Europe provides a particularly dramatic and clear example of the ideological impact of the neo-liberalist housing model on housing systems that are undergoing fundamental re-evaluation by governments. One might have thought that, in the attempt to get away from state socialism, the command economy model of public renting represented by English-speaking countries would have been rejected as repugnant and unacceptable, and the unitary rental market model of the germanic societies adopted instead.

The great asset available to Eastern European countries with regards to the rental market is that they have inherited a large public rental stock after half a century of communism which could form the basis for a cost rental stock. One alternative to selling the dwellings into individual owner occupation would be to sell or transfer the stock to cost rental housing organisations which could be trusts or owned and run by the tenants themselves in the form of tenant rental co-operatives. Ideally the monolithic state rental housing stock would be broken up into a diverse quilt of different types of cost and profit rental housing organisations, in addition to tenant ownership and owner occupied housing. These countries would then possess a mature cost rental stock that would in most cases constitute a ready-made unitary rental market without an extended harmonisation transition.

One response might therefore have been to break up the large estates of state housing into small tenant-managed rental co-operatives and to encourage diversity and competition in the rental market. But policy makers in these societies have not been presented with such alternatives. There has not even been the most cursory investigation of the unitary rental market model as an alternative.

The tragedy of the rush to privatise this state rental stock that has been under way with varying degrees of success in Eastern Europe over the last few years is that this opportunity is being lost. It takes many decades to build up a reasonably mature cost rental housing stock, but only a few years to fritter away the maturation gains by selling them off at what amount to virtual give-away prices.

Instead of the social market model of diversification, the anglo-saxon neo-liberalist model has been promoted as the true representative of genuine free market housing policy. Eastern European countries have therefore rushed headlong into creating the housing conditions most likely to result in the establishment of a residual public rental command economy through the wholesale transference of state rental housing to the ownership of sitting tenants at massively discounted prices – in some cases up to 90 per cent of market values. In just a few short years, the large stock of cost rental housing in many Eastern European countries has been almost entirely dissipated. In a veritable orgy of asset stripping, conversion of much of this stock into owner occupied housing at enormous public expense in lost capital receipts has been forced through as a *fait accompli* with barely any strategic policy debate. The result will be the replacement of one form of monolith, state rental, with another, owner occupation.

There are good power-politics reasons for this state of affairs. In the chaotic emergence from communism, there has been no time as yet for the formation of a properly functioning corporatist power structure. In addition, the first post-communist governments were often elected on platforms of nationalism rather than sectional interests. The sale of public rental housing was seen as a simple and apparently cost-free means of garnering widespread support and minimal opposition. It would seem that no one actually sat down and worked out the cost of heavily discounted sales on the value of state assets, nor its strategic and long-term policy consequences.

This internal political vacuum also laid these countries open to international influence. As already suggested in the introduction, historically, Eastern – or more accurately Central – Europe has been strongly influenced by either the Russian or germanic cultures. German cultural hegemony became deeply entrenched in Central Europe first through the Habsburg Empire and Prussia, and later by Germany. In the century from Bismarck to Hitler the replacement of germanic hegemony in Eastern Europe in 1945 with half a century of Russian hegemony, which suddenly collapsed in 1989 has clearly left Eastern Europe exposed to the full blast of anglo-saxon influence in the transition from communism that has taken place.

The 'German model' based upon constructing an integrated cost and profit rental housing stock, as an entirely post-war innovation, has therefore barely been recognised. It will probably take a couple of decades before growing German power and the resulting increase in German influence is re-established in Eastern Europe. Meanwhile, the rapid reconstitution of East European housing systems along dualistic, or what might be termed 'new command economy' lines has almost been accomplished.

The failure of countries with unitary rental market strategies to explicate the unitary rental market as a clear alternative to the dualist model – itself a result of anglo-saxon influence in those countries – makes it likely that the housing systems of Eastern Europe will become increasingly dualist at least over the next couple of decades. And given the increasing penetration of anglo-saxon perspectives through the English language, the unitary rental model is not even securely established in many countries with unitary rental markets.

However, the long-term structuring of East European rental markets, is far from clear. A growing interest in the unitary rental market cannot be ruled out, particularly if the dualist system causes increasing problems over the coming years. German cultural influence on policy in general remains strong in some countries, such as Hungary (Cox, 1993), while the specific social conditions in Eastern Europe make it likely that no single model imported from abroad will necessarily become fully implemented (Gray, 1993). It is therefore hopefully too early to write off the chances of the social market approach becoming established in at least Poland, the Czech Republic, Slovakia and Hungary, the East European countries that have traditionally been most open to germanic cultural influence.

10 From command economy to the social market

INTRODUCTION

That the dualist rental system in English-speaking countries has remained unquestioned both by policy makers and politicians is something that housing researchers must accept a portion of the responsibility for. They have been largely content to criticise the shortcomings of the existing dominant model in a piecemeal fashion, without questioning the terms of the debate and without reference to the development of a coherent alternative. This accepts the unspoken assumptions that lie behind the neo-liberalist profit market model and so the debate is carried on within implicitly accepted consensual boundaries. The widespread appeal for the abolition of mortgage income tax relief in Britain is a classic example of this.

The reason for this is to be found in the fact that comparative research portrays rental systems as more or less homogeneously in the anglo-saxon mould, even if it is conceded that there are national variations. In the preceding pages I have tried to show that this perspective is flawed and have developed an alternative two-model framework in which an alternative to the anglo-saxon model exists and is a part of practical housing policy in a number of countries.

In this chapter I want to move on from this critical conceptual approach to propose how it might be possible to reconstruct dualist rental systems along unitary lines. Moving from a public rental command economy to a unitary rental market is a major change of policy strategy. It involves profound changes across a wide range of policy fields. It is also a long-term venture, taking several decades to come to fruition. Why should one want to do this? The answers to this question are to be found throughout the preceding chapters, but are worth restating briefly in the context of this chapter.

THE CASE AGAINST DUALISM

The general case against dualism is that it paradoxically leads to greater state intervention in housing than does a unitary rental market. The policy of systematically disavantaging cost rental housing has two distinct dimensions. In the first place, cost rental housing is effectively nationalised and either developed under state control or gradually placed under increasing state control. By this means, cost rental housing is effectivly removed as a potential competitor to profit renting. Second, once a nationalised cost rental sector has been created, increasingly tight centralised political control has to be exercised over cost renting in order to prevent it becoming too popular and too competitive in relation to profit renting and owner occupation.

Largely as a result of this increased state intervention, dualism results in artificially induced housing shortages. Indeed, chronic and extreme housing shortages with resultant widespread homelessness appear to be an integral feature of dualist rental systems. The reasons for this are not difficult to understand. Profit renting has never in any period of history been able to satisfactorily meet the demand for rental housing and when cost renting is structured in such a manner as to limit its availability then rental housing shortages are almost inevitable.

But most important of all, dualism minimises housing choice, by a policy strategy that in effect forces as many households as possible into owner occupation. The choice that is made available to the vast majority of households is that between owner occupation and profit renting. The latter, with its high insecurity of tenure, rents that gravitate towards a return on the current market value of property, and often high levels of landlord selectivity from among potential tenants and interference in domestic matters create a housing system in which the only form of housing that offers security of tenure and at least an element of non-profit extraction is owner occupation. Dualism therefore channels demand into owner occupation.

Some other negative consequences of dualism may be mentioned. Periodic rent differential crises in which central government organises a major policy strategy intervention to tighten control over public renting to prevent it expanding is one. The ratchet effect, whereby subsidies to encourage marginal buyers are increased thereby increasing the relative deprivation of the remaining rump of non-buyers is another. Deepening glut–famine owner occupation market cycles as the home ownership rate rises is yet another. The emergence of a slum owner occupier sector as more low-income earners are forced by the policy strategy to buy is another.

But above all, the case for moving away from a dualist rental system rests upon the suffering that the high degree of compulsion and policy direction it involves places on the lives of ordinary people. The policy abandonment of private renting in the naive belief that the profit-driven market works, combined with the repression of cost renting, is the most effective way that can be devised of restricting the availability of rental housing and thereby limiting choice in housing tenures.

Those to suffer most from this are the poor. Among these must be reckoned the growing number of single-parent households – mostly headed by women. Only a privileged few of these can afford owner occupation, the only housing which, in a dualist system, is both in adequate supply and offers security of tenure.

This chapter is therefore prescriptive and policy orientated. Here I indicate at a strategic level the kinds of policies that are needed in order to achieve a major change in direction for housing policy for a country with a command public rental policy. Examples are taken from more than one English-speaking country.[1]

However, the discussion concentrates particularly on Britain, where the possibilities for a rapid switch from dualism to the unitary market are greatest. There the public rental housing stock is largest and most mature. An additional factor is that British public renting is undergoing large-scale and fundamental changes in its organisation.

These changes have, if nothing else, 'broken the mould' and made housing practitioners and policy makers open to new ideas and changes that have hitherto been undreamed of. Furthermore, although obviously none of the changes are intended to encourage the emergence of a unitary rental market, some of them, such as the diversification of the ownership of the stock, are congruous with, and facilitate the pursuit of, such a strategy.

The discussion has been broken down into a number of aspects of housing and general social policy that need to be changed in major ways in order to achieve the desired result. These include an orderly state disengagement from public renting that nurtures a cost rental sector, policy towards private renting, general housing subsidies, social security, and rent allowances. This decomposition of a policy strategy into a number of discrete measures must not result in losing sight of the overall guiding principles of the policy strategy that hold them together.

RECONSTRUCTING PUBLIC RENTING

There are two principal structural changes that need to be made to public rental housing in order to move from dualism to a unitary rental market. The most important is to extricate public rental housing from political management. This is best achieved by privatising public renting by transferring ownership and control of the stock to non-profit housing organisations. The other change is equally important. This is the fragmentation of ownership both in the number of local operators and in the type of organisations, in order to maximise competition. We may consider these two aspects in turn.

Privatisation: the 'arm's length' company

Privatisation involves the sale or transfer of state-owned assets into private ownership. However, it is commonly understood as transference of ownership into private profit-seeking hands, for example by the creation of a joint-stock company in the British privatisations of industries such as steel and coal and of utilities such as telephone, electricity, water and gas. Occasionally, however, major privatisations do involve transference to non-profit organisations. The creation of hospital trusts in the British National Health Service is one example of this. In education, the privatisation of schools often takes place into non-profit forms, albeit with a strong bias to schooling for the children of the privileged.

The key to the establishment of a unitary rental market must be the creation of a cost rental sector that is capable of operating on the housing market in direct and active competition with profit renting. A practical way of attaining this goal is to convert public renting into cost renting. Public rental housing, with levels of maturation considerably higher than newbuild, provides a ready-made stock of cost rental housing that would establish cost renting on a strong footing by providing a stock of relatively mature housing upon which expansion can be based. Privatisation into non-profit form is therefore the single most important measure in moving towards a unitary rental market.

There are many different forms of privatisation that can be considered. Whichever is adopted it is crucial to extricate public renting from state management. This involves removing strategic managerial decisions about rent levels, investment and vacancy allocations from the political arena. This is most easily done by disentangling public renting from other state activities by reconstituting public renting as trusts or in some other non-profit organisational form.

The key policy difference between command and market policies is that whereas command policies involve government in the month-to-month managerial decisions needed to run a stock of housing, market policy requires a drawing back of state involvement from a management role. The role of government in a market policy is rather to determine the ground rules that govern the management of the stock. That role involves continual monitoring and periodic intervention using market conforming measures to steer the market to more open competition and equality between different providers of rental housing.

Cost rental housing organisations can take many forms. A compromise solution between local or state government housing and private cost rental housing organisations is the 'arm's length company' (Raynsford, 1992). This can take a wide range of forms, from ordinary joint-stock companies in which local government has a majority share or at least a say in the running of the company to explicitly non-profit making housing trusts.

In Sweden cost rental housing organisations are commonly (though by no means universally) housing companies in which the majority of shares are owned by the local government. Such a form retains overall control to ensure the company remains non-profit making but leaves strategic management to the board of directors. It also has the advantage that proper accounts have to be maintained and the finances kept separate from those of the local authority. It has the potential disadvantage that a company is only non-profit making because the local authority wishes it to be so. That is, the organisational form is not constitutionally non-profit making, and could at any time be converted into a profit-seeking operation. For a local authority to do this and use the surpluses for its non-housing needs would be tantamount to levying an extra tax on its tenants.

The trust solution is that adopted in some local authorities in Sweden and in South Australia. This is essentially the same as the company version except that the organisation is non-profit making in its constitution rather than because the local authority, using its majority holding, chooses not to declare a dividend. Experience in Sweden has shown that occasionally local authorities cannot resist extracting surpluses out of their housing companies. This must be a temptation that will grow as the stock of the housing company matures.

Diversifying ownership through stock transfer

The 'arm's length company' arrangement is the minimalist solution to de-politicising the public rental housing stock, since it ensures that local authorities retain overall ownership and ultimate control. A more radical measure that ensures complete removal of local authority control is that of stock transfer to a private landlord. This has been a measure introduced by the British government to reduce the size of the council stock. It is a measure that, like that of creating arm's length companies, can have several different versions, some of which are more in conformity with the concept of the social market than others.

Some transfer has been made to tenant rental co-operatives. However, in general, the British version is relatively unfavourable to the non-profit principle. This should come as no surprise since its primary purpose is not to create a unitary rental market.

The British law therefore gives private landlords sweeping powers to expropriate council housing stock under certain pre-defined circumstances. They may make an offer for a stock of housing – commonly for an estate – and the local authority can be compelled to accept it as long as the purchase price covers outstanding debt and that, after a vote, a majority of tenants do not oppose (as distinct from actively supporting) the transfer. While in theory, transfer can take place to a profit-orientated landlord as well as a non-profit landlord, it is likely that the majority of such transfers will in fact take place to the latter. Nevertheless, this measure provides private landlords with rights and privileges that constitute a landlord version of the right to buy.

It is still early to determine the extent and nature of such transfers. Only a few transfers have taken place and these have all been to non-profit housing organisations, primarily housing associations. Normally, although transfer price has been extremely low, it has been higher than the cost of the outstanding debt that is also transferred. This, of course, decreases the maturity of the transferred stock without any benefit to the tenants of the transferred stock in terms of either a larger stock or modernisation of existing housing. Nor is there any guarantee that the capital realisation made by the council will be to the benefit of the remaining, non-transferring, council tenants. There is, of course, no consideration given in this measure to the impact of such transfers on the debt-structure – and hence on rent pooling – of the remaining stock.

A much more rational stock transfer system aimed at minimising the debt-load and creating a diversity of providers that had housing stocks with similar levels of maturation would be what I would term *profile stock transfers at cost*. That is, the housing authority transfers tranches of its stock, the debt-profiles of which approximately match the debt-profile of the total housing authority stock. Transfer is made to non-profit housing organisations at cost. That is, the buying organisation pays only the outstanding debt on the transferred stock. In this way, a number of cost rental housing organisations can be established – and those that already exist can be strengthened – with a start-up stock of dwellings that have similar levels of maturity to both each other and to the local housing authority.

The end result of profile stock transfers at cost would be to break up the local monopoly of public renting while neither sacrificing the non-profit principle nor widening differences in the levels of maturation of the stocks of different cost rental housing organisations. It is probably not an exaggeration to say that the manner in which the privatisation of the public rental stock takes place is decisive for the creation of a varied and competitive range of small-scale cost rental providers with stocks of housing characterised by the highest possible levels of maturation.

Rent policy

We have seen in Chapter 8 that there are many different systems of rent setting even among the relatively small number of countries where a policy strategy of creating a unitary rental market is being pursued. I do not propose to enter a lengthy discussion over the merits and demerits of different systems. This is not just a space-saving convenience. It is more because all these societies have different power structures and have taken different routes to the unitary rental market accordingly. They also start off from different preconditions that happen to exist at the particular point in time that the decision to move towards the unitary market is taken.

The key common principle that underlies all systems, however, is to maximise the effectiveness of the cost rental sector in holding down market rents. The most important ingredient in this is the ability to use the maturity of the stock to cross-subsidise housing with different use-values and debt-loads. This is done by charging below-cost rents in order to attract households to high-cost housing that is in low demand, and charging above-cost rents to households in low-cost housing that is in high demand. The rent structure of the cost rental housing stock must be demand sensitive in order to attain this.

This demand-sensitive rent pooling differs in important respects from blanket rent pooling systems common in public rental housing systems. Some of the latter may take some account of size, modernity of facilities, level of amenity etc. when setting rents. However, they usually take little or no account of more qualitative factors influencing demand such as locational advantages (including, for example, open spaces, access to shops and the quality of local schools).

Part of the problem is undoubtedly the managerial style that is typical of command economies. The existence of a huge dammed-up demand that results from the suppression of cost renting means that a low premium is placed on the attainment of a demand-sensitive rent structure.

Attempts to develop a demand-sensitive rent structure will therefore often be limited to the construction of formulae to take into account some of the more obviously measurable dimensions of use-value. But exercises in the construction of complex formulae for taking into account a range of weighted factors deemed to be important in determining rents are not the optimal way of arriving at demand-sensitive rents. Such devices only provide a crude and basic first estimate, and must be understood as part of an initial data evaluation.

Demand-sensitive rent setting requires a much more flexible procedure that is managerial in nature and dependent ultimately on the judgement of those responsible for setting rents. Formulae can provide a guide but need to be complemented by information on demand drawn from records of applications for housing by prospective tenants, vacancy rates in different kinds of properties, and other sources that will allow a qualitative decision to be made. This is how the manager of a private profit-orientated housing company would operate and there is no reason to believe that the manager of a cost rental housing organisation would be any worse at this job.

In applying demand sensitivity to rent setting, the principal restriction unique to a cost rental housing organisation is that it needs to balance deficits on low-demand dwellings with surpluses on high-demand dwellings. This means that the more mature the stock is the greater is the ability of the organisation to widen differentials between high- and low-demand housing so as to reflect differences in demand between dwellings.

Immaturity is, of course, the major limitation that an immature stock of cost rental housing places on the possibility of attaining a demand-sensitive rent structure. And it is for this reason that in the early decades, rent regulation is typically used to allocate cost rental housing. In theory there is no reason why rents for very unattractive housing cannot be near or even below zero. In practice, it may be more economical to refurbish, rebuild or even in extreme cases to demolish such housing if demand is so low as to compel the charging of peppercorn rents.

The point at which lowering rents well below costs ceases to be economical is heavily dependent on the nature of the social security system and particularly the manner in which housing allowances are structured. In command systems there is little incentive to charge rents below costs because of the restricted safety-net function of public renting. Command system rent structures commonly do not differentiate sufficiently between different kinds of households and different kinds of housing standards. This is aggravated by the fact that the residualised nature of dualist public renting generates a very restricted and economically weak clientele.

Discounted sales

There is another limitation on the ability of cost rents to be made demand sensitive through pooling. The ability to charge surplus-generating rents on high-demand dwellings is severely limited by the sales policies that are often imposed on cost rental housing organisations by central governments.

Where the organisations themselves are compelled to sell, especially granting large discounts on market prices, any attempt to cross pool rental income from high- to low-demand dwellings is likely to increase rents on attractive dwellings to the point at which it is worthwhile for the tenant to buy the dwelling. Differential cross pooling will, in such a system, trigger the subsidised purchase of the dwelling with its consequent loss to the rental stock.

This, of course, is the intention behind discounted sales. Discounting is normally justified as a compensation to the household which has paid rent for many years. The argument is that having done so and thereby contributed to the growing value of the property the tenants who buy should be recompensed for this. Indeed, in some countries the longer the household has held the tenancy the larger the discount that is granted.

This is, of course, pure rationalisation to justify weakening cost rental housing and favouring owner occupation. Historically, those who have held long tenancies have often been those who have been most heavily subsidised. This is the case both in terms of state subsidies and in subsidies accruing as a result of rent pooling.

State subsidies have been historically high during the early post-war decades. It is only in recent years that they have begun to fall significantly in most countries. More seriously, where rent pooling has been in effect, the tenancy of a newly built dwelling in 1950 has commonly been in receipt of a net subsidy paid by the tenants of an older dwelling. Discounted sale will therefore compound a new subsidy on top of two previous generous subsidies that may have been paid over many decades.

It is equity between buying and non-buying tenants that is most seriously violated by a policy of discounted sales. The tenants of a new dwelling will commonly be subsidised through rent pooling for decades. Sooner or later – depending on the rate of maturation – this subsidy will fall to zero and then become negative, as what is now an older dwelling is in turn being used to cross-subsidise new dwellings.

One might reasonably argue that, far from giving buying tenants a discount based on the length of the tenancy, tenants who happily accept cross-pooling subsidies while the dwelling is relatively new should not, once their dwelling has aged and it is their turn to cross-subsidise, be allowed to remove the dwelling from the stock by buying it at a discount. Indeed, there may be a good case to be made out for charging a *premium* for those who wish to buy once their dwelling moves out of being a net recipient of cross-pool subsidies.

This is the main reason why the attempts by the central state or local government to compel cost rental housing organisations to sell cost rental housing at a discount to tenants or indeed to any person or organisation must be ceased during any transition to a unitary market. Future sales must be made on a purely commercial basis as deemed beneficial to the organisation's own tenants.

For a cost rental housing organisation this means that the sale price needs normally to be at replacement cost. However, dwellings which, because of low demand, command a rent below costs may often be deemed desirable to sell at a discount to reflect the fact that the rental income it generates is insufficient to cover its costs.

The sale of dwellings at a discount is arguably one of the most iniquitous aspects of the whole dualist strategy of discriminating against cost renting. The attempt to justify it in moral terms turns all logic on its head. The fact that it has been so widely unquestioned is a tribute to the hegemonic position of dualist policy strategy in so many countries.

THE ROLE OF PROFIT RENTING

Profit-orientated rental housing is not a necessary component of a unitary rental market. Whether profit renting has a role in a future unitary rental market or not depends upon the type of policy strategy that is pursued. A unitary rental market in which cost renting dominates the market will be quite different from one in which cost renting leads or influences it. However, following the principle that the more varied the supply, the more the competition that will result, the existence of profit-orientated rental provision is arguably advantageous.

In any event, moving from a dualist system to a unitary market is likely to be more widely accepted politically if profit renting is retained as an integral part of the rental market.

The choice of policy strategy will also be influenced by the particular circumstances and nature of the rental system that is to be reformed. This depends in part on the size and nature of the private rental market being transformed. In the USA, Canada, Australia and New Zealand private renting accounts for around 20 per cent of dwellings and the public rental sectors are much smaller. In such countries the situation is rather similar to that in many European countries immediately after the war.

The strategy here might be to encourage the emergence of a range of small cost rental housing providers through start-up subsidies. In addition, breaking up the state housing monopolies by making profile stock transfers at cost from these state monopolies to the new cost rental housing organisations would accelerate the maturation of the new cost rental organisations. The aim would be to develop cost rental provision to a level of maturation that will enable it at the earliest possible opportunity to compete with profit renting.

But such an approach would not work everywhere. In Britain, for example, the private rental sector is very small, accounting for only some 6 per cent of dwellings. This makes it harder – though not necessarily impossible – to create a mixed cost/profit rental market.

But the size of the profit rental sector is not the only factor to consider. The type of profit renting that exists is also of importance. Dualist rental systems in countries with high rates of owner occupation are likely to have private rental sectors that are heavily influenced by the owner occupied sector. Two examples of such influence can be given here.

One is the emergence of a large stratum of low-income owner occupiers who sublet rooms or a flat in their owner occupied housing in order to be able to afford to pay the mortgage (see Chapter 4). This owner occupier (or petty) landlordism is not amenable to commercial rental operations due to the primary concern with retaining the right to reclaim full possession of the property. A central concern of such landlords is therefore both preventing tenants from gaining security of tenure by granting only short-term leases and the highly personalised nature of such landlordism that places severe restrictions on who may or may not be acceptable as a tenant living in the same house as the landlord.

The leasehold provisions of such housing are often draconian and verge on constituting violations of basic human rights. No children or pets is a common condition of being granted short-term and insecure tenure, and some leases even specify that musical instruments should not be kept (let alone played) at the property and that the dwelling should not be used for political or religious meetings. Where a large proportion of private renting comprises this kind of landlordism it may be that there is very little commercial landlordism upon which to build a viable commercial profit rental sector.

The other way in which large owner occupied sectors infuence the nature of the private rental sector is the way in which the heavy subsidisation of owner occupation boosts prices of owner occupied housing. The subsidies become capitalised in the value of the house through the manner in which subsidies increase demand for owner occupied housing. This in turn impacts on the valuation of rental property, increasing the minimum rental income that is considered necessary to generate a return on the investment that matches the returns on alternative forms of investment. The result of this will often be that renting ceases to be an attractive form of investment and the supply of rental housing falls. The overall effect of a large subsidised owner occupied housing market is therefore to reduce the demand for rental housing.

In a well functioning rental market where there is a reasonable degree of security of tenure the price of rental property will reflect the rental income it is able to generate. Vacant possession price will play a marginal part in determining values. In a residential property market dominated by heavily subsidised owner occupier housing vacant possession prices will be more important in determining the market value of rental property and the high level of subsidisation of owner occupied housing will make it worth while to sell rental housing into owner occupation. Another way of putting this is that the owner occupied housing market penetrates the rental market to such an extent as to undermine the autonomy of the latter. This is one important factor in the drastic decline of private renting in home owning societies with dualist rental systems.

The kind of short-term opportunistic profit renting that tends to be associated with owner occupation may have a role to fulfil in providing temporary rental housing for a specialist market of students, foreign visitors and those seeking temporary housing, for example as a result of divorce. However, it cannot reasonably be expected to provide permanent rental housing.[2] The encouragement of a profit rental sector therefore requires more than just measures to encourage profit renting in general. It requires that thought be given to the encouragement of a commercially orientated form of landlordism that can become an organic part of a larger mixed cost/profit rental market that operates with similar long-term investment and development planning.

This suggests in turn that the kind of landlords most appropriate for operating on an integrated rental market will be institutional landlords. These will be companies or subsidiary companies to banks, building societies and insurance companies (for example), that are able to provide a reliable and impersonal service to tenants and that will view their properties as long-term investments rather than a means of eking out a pension or low income merely to tide owner occupiers over a difficult phase of the household life-cycle.

The decision to encourage profit renting must therefore be made in the context of a clear understanding of the difference between investor landlords and petty landlords and the different kinds of rental provision by these. Once this is understood, subsidies or other incentives can be formed in such a way as to direct them to permanent investor landlords rather than to owner occupier or petty landlords.

SUBSIDIES

The general international trend to reducing subsidies should not be understood simply as the product of a neo-liberalist reaction. There are good reasons why subsidies can be phased out in many countries at this particular point in time.

The major expansion of the housing stock that occupied the first few decades of the post-war period must be seen in historical perspective as fairly unique. A major depression sandwiched between two world wars led to increasingly acute housing shortages. These were made all but desperate by residential war devastation, followed by a quarter of a century of almost continuous economic expansion. As if this were not enough, in a number of countries, including Australia and Sweden, rapid urbanisation and industrialisation extended well into the post-war period and created large-scale migration both from the countryside and abroad.

The early post-war decades were therefore a period in which the cost rental stocks of many countries expanded rapidly. Front loading was heavy and stocks were disproportionately made up of new housing. Heavy subsidisation was therefore essential if housing was to be built that could be rented out to ordinary households in the numbers required.

Since the 1970s these conditions no longer pertain. New constructions have fallen significantly, accelerating the maturation of an already maturing stock of cost rental housing. This has been further aided by high rates of house price inflation during much of the late post-war period. Given these dramatically different circumstances it is not at all surprising that subsidies are being reduced quite substantially in many countries.

However, it is clear that levels of subsidy cannot be directly correlated with the extent of shortages and the degree of maturation of the stock. Subsidies are also used as a policy instrument to favour certain forms of tenure and to discriminate against others.

Thus, for example, in order to develop a unitary rental market it is often necessary to engage in the equivalent of 'positive discrimination'. This is done in order to encourage the emergence of a cost rental sector while its housing stocks are immature so that they can become sufficiently established to compete with profit renting. Once this has been attained subsidies can then be phased out to remove such positive discrimination.

More commonly, subsidies are used to maintain a dualist rental market by encouraging owner occupation. In this case the subsidy weapon can be used in two different ways. It can be used to subsidise owner occupation, in which case the subsidy weapon is used as a market-subverting device by disadvantaging the competition. This is not done as as part of a wider policy to establish equal grounds for all tenures but rather as a means of encouraging the dominance of owner occupation in the housing sector as a whole. The subsidy weapon can also be used in the form of a negative subsidy, or implicit tax, on cost renting to undermine its competitiveness.

Given the above types of subsidy biases in a dualist rental system, the transition to a unitary rental market will require a re-alignment of the subsidy system in a number of respects. Whether subsidies to the cost rental sector will be needed depends in part on how badly damaged its maturity has become as a result of measures taken in response to previous rent-differential crises. This will clearly vary from country to country. Where there has been chronic neglect of repairs and maintenance and where there is a need to expand supply considerably, it might be necessary to provide subsidies to aid the recuperation and recovery of the stock from the damage of the preceding command policies.

In addition, in some countries it will be necessary to revert to the previous system of paying housing allowances for public tenants out of the social security budget instead of out of public rent surpluses. A return to cost-covering rents would in any event be a necessary reform, and a consequence of this would be to shift the burden of housing allowances from the small group of least disavantaged cost tenants to the public exchequer.

This would also reinstate tenure neutrality between households in terms of housing allowances between cost renting, profit renting and owner occupation. It is only in public renting that in some countries the better-off households are expected to pay the housing allowances of the least well-off. In owner occupation and private renting, housing allowances are paid out of exchequer social security commitments rather than being paid for by those profit rental tenants or owner occupiers who are not eligible for housing allowances.

Another change in housing subsidies that would be an essential component of moving towards a housing system where household choice is not steered by government preferences would be to move towards the tenure neutrality of subsidies in broadest possible terms. In dualist systems this usually involves reducing tax breaks and other subsidies to owner occupiers, or increasing subsidies to cost renting and possibly also private renting so that per capita subsidies to households in different tenures are not biased. The aim here is to disengage governments from attempting to steer household choice into one or another form of tenure, so that household choice can determine the relative size of each, as free from government interference as possible.

A relatively painless way to accomplish this transition would be to accept as a given starting point the current levels of subsidy to owner occupiers. This could then be taken as the yardstick used to determine the dimension of subsidies to cost rental tenants in such a way that matches subsidies to owner occupiers. It would be difficult to motivate lower levels of subsidy for cost rental tenants than are available for owner occupiers and an open political discussion on this point could only be beneficial in removing the last vestiges of stigma attached to cost renting in relation to owner occupation.

HOUSING ALLOWANCES

Quite apart from shifting the burden of housing allowances from cost rental tenants back to the public exchequer, the structure of the housing allowance system is an additional matter that needs attention. In Chapter 5 we observed that dualist systems tend to be associated with minimalist welfare state provision and that the residualised safety-net mentality that governs the construction of the housing sectors of such societies is paralleled in other areas of the welfare state.

One problem with the construction of housing allowances in such societies is that they tend to be *marktinkonform*. This results from the fact that they are constructed in such a manner as to minimise their cost. This means in practice that they bring tenants up to a minimum level irrespective of the level of rent but in such a manner as to make little difference how high rents are. Housing allowances are therefore often very limited in availability – that is they have low income eligibility ceilings – while at the same time they have low levels of discrimination between different levels of rent and different sizes and types of household. This has the effect of making household demand relatively insensitive to variations in rent levels.

The reason that demand sensitivity in rental housing allowances tends to be low is that demand sensitivity is not a priority in a system where allocations are made administratively and without regard to demand, as is the case in a public rental command economy. Demand sensitivity is much more important in a competitive cost rental sector.

The most important consequence of demand insensitivity is in the public rental sector, where the housing allowance system acts as a countervailing force to the expression of household demand. This is in part a deliberate and well-meaning attempt to create greater equality.

However, it has the effect of deterring demand-sensitive rent pooling by cost rental housing organisations. This does not matter very much in a form of rental provision that is highly restricted in access and where the proportion of households eligible for housing allowance is very high – up to three-quarters or more. It does, however, have negative implications, even in a command economy.

One consequence of this demand insensitivity is the existence of huge imbalances in demand for public rental or cost rental housing. Housing that is attractive and in high demand will have long waiting lists for allocation, while unattractive housing will have high or even very high vacancy rates. This phenomenon is apparent even in the administrative allocation systems of command public renting. There is even an administrative concept – 'hard-to-let' – to describe this latter kind of housing.

It is a supreme irony that the very measures that are brought in with the intention of minimising social inequality end up by perpetuating and even accentuating it. It is therefore important that, as part of a transition from dualism to a unitary rental market, the housing allowance system be reconstituted in such a way as to make it maximally *marktkonform*.

This involves designing a housing allowance system that is based on norms governing the standard of housing that is minimally acceptable

for different sizes and types of household given rents that match current cost-covering levels. Beyond these limits, housing allowances
would be tapered. The impact of the system should be to ensure that
housing allowances cover minimum needs but that use-values over
and above this have to be paid for increasingly by the households
themselves.

HOUSING AND OTHER AREAS OF SOCIAL POLICY

The transition to a unitary rental market cannot be considered
entirely divorced from other areas of social policy. Rental policy strategy impinges upon other areas of social policy because underlying
these other areas are longer-term policy strategies that inform their
structuring. To take a simple example, English-speaking countries
have social security systems that are based on safety-net principles.
So their social security provision will be coloured by this as part of a
long-term policy strategy in the spirit of the Roosevelt/Beveridge
approach.

A rental policy strategy of residualising cost renting is easier to
pursue if parallel processes of residualisation of non-profit forms are
taking place in other areas such as health, education, social security,
pensions and transport.

Housing allowances provide a case in point. These have been
designed to fit into a broader system of social security. In a social security system based on a residualised welfare concept of supplementary
benefits the scope and population coverage of housing allowances will
be similarly restricted. The housing allowance system will synchronise
with the social security system, and will mirror its aims. This will result
in a housing allowance system that is similarly residual in nature.

This synergy is an important dimension to the strategic policy
structuring of the rental system. It is too complex and far-reaching
to deal with in passing as an afterthought to direct rental policy
issues. This will therefore be discussed further in the following, final
chapter.

11 Wider issues: housing and the welfare state

INTRODUCTION

A book of this sort inevitably raises a number of implications that extend the discussion beyond traditional housing studies and integrate housing issues into wider social policy. One of these – the relationship between housing allowances and social security – was indicated at the end of the preceding chapter. The importance of relating policy strategy in different social policy fields to one another is that it is only by so doing that the long-term structuring of the welfare state can be understood.

Such wider issues cannot possibly be dealt with adequately without considerable dispersal of effort, and loss of focus. In this final chapter, I want to explore and point to ways in which they can be developed and followed up. In one sense, then, this chapter can be read as the prologue to a further separate study of housing and the welfare state.

I do not attempt to cover the whole area of housing. My primary concern is the relationship between those dimensions of housing that are directly affected by rental policy strategy. In particular, I am interested in the different synergies that are created by dualist and unitary systems in relation to other areas of social policy.

HOUSING AND OTHER AREAS OF SOCIAL POLICY

The relationship between housing allowances and other areas of social security places limits on both the scale and the structuring of the housing allowance system, when planning a shift in rental policy strategy. In this section I propose to examine the relationship between housing and other areas of social policy to indicate the complexity of these relationships.

I am particularly concerned with dimensions of housing that are central to distinguishing dualist from unitary rental strategies. These include the balance between owning and renting in a society, the manner in which the rental system is organised and the extent to which rents are cost based.

The discussion is far from exhaustive, either in terms of the areas of social policy that have been chosen for illustration, or in the ways in which rental strategy dimensions of housing interact with each chosen area of social policy. They are intended primarily to be illustrative of the complex inter-relationship between housing and other social policy areas.

Housing and pensions

Housing comprises a large proportion of household expenditure. The differences in patterns of life-cycle expenditure between owner occupation and renting are also very substantial. The cost of owner occupied housing is heavily skewed towards the early years of the life-cycle. In a society with a dualist rental system and concomitant high rates of owner occupation this synergy will impact in a major way on patterns of consumption.

The impact of high rates of owner occupation on the life-cycle distribution of household expenditure is a complex and many-faceted issue. It is not possible in this discussion to explore more than one dimension of it. I therefore propose to look at certain issues around the interaction between owner occupation and pensions.

One of the most striking characteristics of owner occupation is that it redistributes the cost of housing from the middle aged and elderly to the young. The life-cycle housing costs of owner occupation are high in the early years and fall very substantially in old age, when housing is often debt free, and, moreover, maintenance can be neglected, thus passing on the cost of this to the next generation.

The low cost of housing for elderly owner occupiers means that in a society with high rates of home ownership general state pension levels can be lower than would be the case in a society with a large proportion of renting households. This in turn means that it is possible to hold down retirement pensions to a level which could sustain an owner occupier at subsistence, while providing supplementary benefits for the minority of elderly who are tenants.

This saving is, however, illusory, since it is the product of a rescheduling of the cost of housing from the elderly to the young. Moreover, the saving derives from a substantial disinvestment in housing by the older generation. The public savings on pensions is made by the problem of disrepair being passed on to the next generation, partly in the form of a lower inheritance value of the property but also to first-time buyers, who will often be prepared to buy and live in dilapidated properties.

But as we have noted, in a dualist rental system it is precisely newly formed young households who require the heaviest subsidisation to make possible entry into owner occupation. In such a rental system, the only tenure where both security of tenure and at least a proportion of historic costs are available is owner occupation. The public 'savings' on pensions are therefore needed to subsidise entry into owner occupation for marginal first-time buyers.

The financial savings in one area are therefore likely to be needed to make good deficiencies in other areas. In cost renting, the neglect of maintenance is unlikely to be a correlate of old age as it is in owner occupation, as cost rental organisations will commonly have a rolling programme of repairs, maintenance and renovation. It is more likely that in a society where owner occupation is the dominant form of tenure state expenditure is shifted from the elderly to the first time buyer, as an adaptive reaction to the manner in which owner occupation restructures the life-cycle resources of households.

Housing and health insurance

Another example is the relationship between health insurance and housing. Shifting the burden of financing health care from a universal national system to the individual may result in the reduction of general tax levels. However, household expenditure may not be reduced as taxation will often be replaced by contributions to private health insurance schemes.

A dualist rental system may distort this redistribution, because of the economic pressure on the large numbers of marginal first-time buyers that exist in a dualist system. For example, young child-free couples, who tend to have few health problems, may choose to gamble on their not needing health insurance by foregoing insurance cover until they have children (when health care needs increase considerably) to enable them to meet their high housing costs.

Housing pressures of this kind will therefore further weaken the collective sharing of the cost of health care, shifting the financial burden from the healthy majority to those social groups prone to illness or in need of medical care. The housing pressures that high rates of owner occupation induce will tend to be fragmenting and anti-collective. These pressures may well reinforce fragmenting and anti-collective tendencies in other areas of social policy. However, this is not always the case. In some areas of social policy, the effect may by quite the opposite.

Housing and study loans

The shift from financing higher education by grants to loans may well have unintended housing consequences. In countries with high rates of owner occupation young households need to concentrate all their financial resources on buying housing. A study loan system undermines this requirement. The loans needed to finance a three or four year first degree course, not to mention higher degrees, amount to a substantial unsecured loan that must make access to owner occupied housing more difficult.

The study loan system is much less damaging in this sense in countries with unitary rental markets, particularly those in which rents are close to or at cost-covering levels. One of the consequences of introducing study loans in countries with dualist rental systems may well be, therefore, to increase the pressure to further subsidise marginal and first-time buyers, thereby counteracting the revenue savings of the study loan system.

Analysis of inter-sector synergy in social policy of the kinds illustrated above is almost entirely lacking. Too much social policy analysis specialises in single areas of social policy, such as health, education and housing, without attempting to uncover the interactions between them.

As a result of this, policy analysts are not very good at advising policy makers on how new policy strategies can be developed. For policy strategies, unlike simplistic single-issue policies are much more prone to unpredictable interactive consequences.

The onus therefore lies on researchers to develop interactive analyses of multiple-policy issues. One useful way of developing this would be to choose one social problem and analyse the interactive impact of several major policy areas upon it. Ultimately, the aim must be to develop explanatory models of how entire national welfare systems operate as interactive wholes.

HOUSING AND THE WELFARE STATE

The impact of the interaction between social policy areas has, of course, been even more neglected in terms of international comparisons of the structuring of the welfare state. Comparative analysis has tended until recently to concentrate on measuring the gross amounts spent by governments on different programmes. Following Wilensky (1975) societies with high levels of public expenditure are deemed to be 'leaders' and those with low levels are deemed to be 'laggards' in terms of the development of the welfare state.

It is only recently that attempts have been made to develop typologies of welfare states that go beyond quantifying gross national levels of public expenditure. Most promising, Esping-Andersen (1990) has begun to distinguish between different forms of organisation in welfare systems. Such work is, however, as we have seen in Chapter 5, still in its infancy and extremely crude.

More sophisticated analyses, including determining the interactions that exist between sectors comprising welfare systems remain an almost completely uncharted area of research. We have barely been aware of the issues involved, let alone begun to formulate the appropriate questions that need to be asked.

Here I want to begin the task of spelling out some of the issues that are involved in understanding the dynamics that sustain the development of, or impel the degeneration of, systems of welfare. My concern is more to suggest fruitful lines of inquiry than to provide answers.

Welfare systems must be understood as dynamic entities rather than as merely somewhat disjointed and essentially inert assemblages of welfare policies. Biologists are increasingly coming to understand the earth as a complex organism in its own right – *Gaia*. A similar perspective will, I believe, be needed in social analysis, and particularly in terms of understanding the structuring and restructuring of welfare states.

An early task in reconceptualising the comparative analysis of welfare states must be to distinguish between different types of welfare system. At the same time, conceiving of welfare states as dynamic wholes made up of interactive policy areas underlines their inherent instability and malleability. Types of welfare systems are not then seen as set in concrete.

Studying processes of transformation from one system to another can then add considerably to our understanding of the kinds of changes needed in discrete areas of welfare that are likely to lead to repercussions in other areas. These in turn may, cumulatively, result in a more strategic re-orientation of the welfare system.

But even such a radical change in approach will not be sufficient. We need to understand *why* certain systems of welfare tend to emerge in some countries but not others, as well as under what conditions they may change. This in turn forces us to examine the structures of power in society. We are likely to find that ultimately systems of welfare are held in place by the compromises and understandings that derive from particular balances of power between interest groups.

I wish to argue that in studying this structuring and restructuring of welfare systems, housing is a key area in the construction of welfare states. The neglect of housing in studies of welfare systems is quite remarkable. Wilensky (1975) explicitly omits housing from his analysis on the grounds that it is too complex an area and interpenetrates other areas of welfare in ways that make it difficult to disentangle and analyse on its own (for a discussion see Kemeny, 1992a, Ch. 5).

This complexity and the embedded nature of housing in social structure and in other social policy areas is, however, precisely my point. It is this that makes the study of housing a vital element in attempting to understand systems of welfare. Interestingly, Esping-Andersen (1990) also has little to say about the organisation of housing.

Yet the neglect of housing in comparative welfare research is strangely at odds with the widespread perception among researchers that housing is a central dimension of inequality and the distribution of resources in society. The 'housing classes' thesis (Rex and Moore, 1967) received considerable attention during the 1970s and early 1980s. It is now out of favour, though the fact that it was ever seriously considered is a reflection of the widespread appreciation among researchers of the centrality of housing to social structure.

The argument continues in a different form in the role of housing in sustaining consumption cleavages. Saunders (1990) points to housing as a key area of consumption cleavages in modern society – or at least in countries that I would identify as possessing dualist rental systems. Saunders divides society into the mass of 'haves' in which owner occupation is a key attribute and a substantial underclass of 'have-nots', largely comprised of public tenants.

Awareness of the importance of housing extends to welfare analysis. Torgersen (1987) identifies housing as 'the wobbly pillar of the welfare state'. He points out that most key areas of social policy, such as education, health, pensions, unemployment benefits and basic income maintenance, are seen as fundamental rights in most industrialised societies, that should unquestionably be organised in national systems of universal provision. The right of every citizen to housing is more ambiguous and equivocal.

Housing lies in a grey zone between the 'universals' of the welfare state and major consumer goods, of which housing is far and away the most important – in a class of its own. In some countries housing is treated more like a 'universal' while in others it is treated more like a consumer good. Similarly, housing has a tendency to change status in this regard within societies over time. This, according to Torgersen, explains the remarkable diversity of housing policies in industrial society.

Torgersen's observation helps us to understand a central paradox in welfare research. This is that, whilst most observers are agreed that housing is a major dimension of welfare, comparative welfare analysts from Wilensky to Esping-Andersen have shied away from placing housing alongside other major policy areas at the centre of their concerns.

Housing, it would seem, is the wild card; the joker in the pack of welfare policy areas. It is the morpheus policy area, capable of taking on an almost bewildering variety of different forms. It can do this precisely because housing is both a consumer good of unique importance and durability and because of its centrality to the organisation of social security.

This characteristic puts housing in a unique position in relation to society and social policy. How it is organised will have far-reaching repercussions throughout society in general and the welfare system in particular.

The ability of housing to structure the lives of ordinary people is profound. Two simple examples will suffice to illustrate this. The first is how the process of urbanisation is accomplished. If it is done by building predominantly detached houses rather than flats, this will determine – effectively for all time – whether a country's urban areas are low or high density. This, in turn, will determine the balance between use of the private car or collective transport. The second example is that given earlier, of the impact of owner occupation on redistributing life-cycle housing costs.

The centrality of housing and its ability to impact on the entire gamut of social relations, its flexibility and the different ways in which it can be provided, and the complex interplay between housing and other social policy areas combine to give housing a unique status in determining the form in which a society and its welfare provision are organised.

For these reasons, housing can be identified as a *strategic policy area* (Kemeny, 1992c). Major changes in policy strategy in housing that are sustained over several decades – such as adopting a dualist or unitary rental policy, or shifting the emphasis of new construction from one dwelling type such as houses to another such as flats – have major implications for the success or failure of other policy areas.

The political control of the housing agenda will be a central plank in any far-reaching attempt to reform the welfare state. This is partly why changes in rental policy strategy by new incoming governments such as have been noted in Australia, New Zealand, Britain, and Sweden cannot be seen as having narrow housing aims.

The onslaught by the British Conservative government on council housing since 1979 must be understood in this context. The 1980s were not only a historic juncture in rental policy strategy. They must be understood as part of a more far-reaching attempt to influence the structuring of welfare provision in general. In that broader welfare policy strategy, attempts to reform housing in general and rental policy in particular have been of central importance.

I would argue that in the long run undermining the viability and competitiveness of cost rental housing is the key to moving towards a highly residualised anglophone settler model of welfare provision. Politicians who wish to achieve this are clearly aware of this, even if they are unable or unwilling to articulate it explicitly.

But this coin has two sides. Reformist movements that wish to develop viable and stable comprehensive welfare states need to be aware that a prime policy target must be the rental system. It is insufficient to merely attempt to increase the size of the public rental sector, as has always been the policy of Britain's Labour Party. We have seen that even a public rental sector of more than 33 per cent of dwellings was no defence against residualisation.

What is needed to strengthen a comprehensive welfare state is not a dualist rental system with a larger cost rental sector but a change in the structure of the rental system from dualism to the unitary rental market. Only when reformers realise this simple fact can an attempt to achieve a shift in welfare strategy have a reasonable chance of success.

Summary and conclusions

INTRODUCTION

The principal message of this book is simple but the arguments that underly it are complex and have implications far beyond the immediate subject matter. For this reason I propose to draw together the arguments and present the disparate elements in a summarised form.

In this book I have concentrated on two issues. The first, and primary, objective is to develop a conceptual framework for understanding the dynamics of rental markets in industrialised societies and the manner in which they develop over time in response to varying policy strategies. An essential dimension of this task is to escape from the anglo-saxon paradigm that dominates comparative research on rental systems.

A second – though by no means secondary – task has been to draw out some of the implications of the dominant anglo-saxon paradigm with the aim of freeing up debate over alternative models. A third issue, only discussed in an exploratory manner, has been the reasons for the emergence of different rental markets in terms of different systems of power and different kinds of welfare regimes.

CRITIQUE OF EXISTING WORK

A key aim of this book is to reassert the centrality of strategic government policy to the structuring of rental housing markets and through this the wider housing system, particularly the balance between the tenures. The growing theoretical awareness of housing researchers over the last two decades has had one major disadvantage as far as developing a clearer understanding of how the rental market operates. This stems from the reaction by housing researchers against narrow policy research.

That reaction led to the argument that government policy towards housing is an epiphenomenon and that the movers and shakers of the housing world are not to be found in the realm of politics and policy making but among wider societal forces – construction companies, financiers, land speculators, and the dynamics of class and economy – which shape the housing market and force public policy to dance to a predetermined tune.

The criticism that there has been too much emphasis upon housing policy is valid to the extent that the detailed shifts and changes in public policy that much policy research is concerned with are not of great moment in understanding how the housing market is structured. However, the broad strategic drift of housing policy in response to changes in the debt structure of cost rental housing over decades and generations is another matter.

The rejection of policy analysis has led to the unquestioned dominance of a form of structural determinism in which abstract market forces have in some unexplicated manner resulted in the trends and tendencies which we see today in the rental markets of many industrialised countries. The sense of inevitability of such trends and their irreversibility is strengthened by the argument that government policy is an irrelevance in affecting them, and in so doing reinforces the anglo-saxon perspective by de-politicising it and presenting it as largely apolitical and the result of impersonal 'market' forces.

I maintain that – in direct contrast to such arguments – policy strategy in its broadest sense is of vital importance in determining the long-term structuring of the housing market. It is therefore a central element in my argument that the reaction against political determinism has grossly distorted our understanding of how housing markets operate and that housing policy at the broad strategic level is fundamental in moulding and forming the housing markets of all industrialised societies.

It follows from this that the ideologies that inform different policy strategies, together with the power structures that generate them, must constitute central subjects for research on the development of different policy strategies towards rental markets. Indeed, it is in large part because the ideological principles that lie behind one or another rental market policy strategy are often left unexplicated and form part of a wider taken-for-granted ideological dominance, that researchers have failed to recognise the existence of policy strategies.

Instead of this, researchers have carried out their analyses from within a dominant and unspoken consensus. The ideological framework that should have been the subject of analysis has instead been a conceptual straitjacket that has impoverished comparative rental housing analysis.

Given the cultural dominance of English-speaking countries in a Cold War and post-Cold War world where international communication is dominated by the English language and its cultural meanings, it is therefore not particularly surprising that the dualist policy strategy should become part of the taken-for-granted perspective of researchers on comparative renting. For language is not merely a neutral medium of communication. It is essentially the linguistic expression of the dominant ideologies that reflect the embedded meanings in – and are constituent to – the cultural form.

When looking at other societies it therefore becomes 'natural' to interpret other cultures through the familiar lenses of ideological concepts taken from home, such as 'residualisation', 'free markets', and 'public rental housing'. The specific and loaded cultural meanings of such concepts are then applied to situations which are qualitatively different, leading to ethnocentric interpretations that generate a comforting, though profoundly misleading, familiarity.

The supreme irony becomes apparent when dualist ideology lays claim to a moral monopoly such as the championship of the 'free' rental market. Research that, by its silent consent, reinforces such a blatant distortion thereby becomes part of the problem of comparative rental housing analysis rather than part of its solution.

Rectifying this state of affairs is an essential first step to reconstituting comparative rental housing research such that it escapes ethnocentricity and becomes capable of generating theories of social change that help us to understand wider processes of change in industrial societies. The twofold framework presented in this study must be seen as an initial attempt to escape from given research agendas and to begin to formulate an alternative. Hopefully, this framework will soon become refined or new and more sensitive ones develop.

MODELS OF RENTAL SYSTEMS

In place of the existing dominant implicit anglo-saxon paradigm I have developed a model of rental system organisation that is based on different strategic policy structurings of the interaction between cost rental and profit rental forms of housing provision. Underlying this model is the interaction between fundamental processes of economic change that all rental housing is subject to – that of maturation – and changes in the direction of policy strategy towards the rental system.

I identify two principal models of organising rental systems. The anglo-saxon model is based on nationalising cost rental housing and segregating it off from profit renting to prevent it competing with profit renting on the open market. This eventually creates two diverging forms of rental housing provision in a system that I term dualist.

Encouraging the integration of cost renting into the market so that it competes directly with profit renting comprises the other model that I term a unitary rental strategy. This is most common among German-speaking countries and countries neighbouring on Germany that had experienced strong German cultural influence before the Second World War.

Each model is associated with different policy problems of management. Maintaining dualist systems requires that the maturation process of public renting be countered to contain its growth. This policy of suppression leads to the instituting of tighter state control and the emergence of a command policy in public renting.

Limiting the availability of cost rental housing effectively forces the great majority of households to choose between insecure and high rent profit renting on the one hand and owner occupation on the other. The result is a rapid expansion of owner occupation. The swollen owner occupied sector that results from dualism also causes policy problems, notably the amplification of glut–famine cycles as more marginal buyers are created and increasing pressure to subsidise entry to owner occupation by low-income earners and their ability to stay in tenure.

By contrast, managing the transition to a unitary market leads to the need to handle the harmonisation of cost and profit rents until full integration can be attained. This will involve slowly phasing out rent regulation and freeing up competition between cost and profit renting. The market distortions that arise from such an extended transition expose the policy strategy to criticism and to pressure to remove all regulation and create a dualist rental system.

There is another difference between dualist and unitary rental systems. The former appear to manifest a narrow range of diversity. The principal difference between dualist systems appears to be the size of the two rental tenures. In contrast, unitary rental markets are highly diverse and varied. No two countries have adopted the same approach to developing an integrated rental market.

More research is needed on the dynamics of unitary rental markets, and, indeed, on the long-term management of dualist systems. In the latter case this involves studies of the command policies that are employed to control and suppress cost renting.

CONCLUSIONS

I am fully aware that the perspective I have developed here is controversial and departs radically from the dominant and traditional research agenda in comparative rental housing research. It disturbs the placid unanimity of a field in housing in which there are no theories or concepts, and no discordant debates or critiques. Instead, housing researchers continue year after year to accumulate empirical data in ever-greater detail. Those data operate to confirm and validate an over-arching consensus.

Greater sensitivity to theoretical questions concerning the analysis of rental markets can hopefully form the basis for greater awareness by policy makers of the alternatives that are available. In particular, awareness is needed that the rental policies of English-speaking countries are not so market orientated as they are made out to be. Genuine free market competition between cost and profit rental housing provides an alternative, more enlightened, and in the long run more problem free, alternative to the dualist command economy in cost rental housing.

Glossary of concepts

command policy: the policy of segregating cost renting off into a state-controlled rental sector

cost renting: a form of rental provision in which rents cover no more than expenditure

demand-sensitive rent pooling: cross-subsidising the rents of housing in low and high demand to match demand to supply on a non-profit basis

dualist rental system: a rental system in which cost renting is not allowed to compete with profit renting for households

glut–famine amplification: the tendency for the glut–famine cycle in the owner occupation housing market to become more accentuated when the proportion of marginal owner occupiers rises

historic juncture: the co-occurrence of the emergence of substantial rent differentials between profit and cost renting and a change in policy strategy

market policy: the policy of integrating cost and profit renting into a single rental market

maturation: the process whereby the average per dwelling cost of debt-servicing a stock of dwellings falls in relation to the cost of debt-servicing new dwellings

maturation index: a measure of the ratio between average debt per dwelling on the existing stock and average debt per newly acquired dwelling

owner occupier landlordism: a type of on-the-premises petty land-lordism that becomes more common as home ownership rates increase

petty landlordism: see owner occupier landlordism

policy constructivism: a perspective in which rental systems are seen as the result of long-term strategic policy making

policy strategy: a long-term set of policy principles guided by a set of assumptions about how markets function

profile stock transfers at cost: the transfer of a representative cross section of a stock of dwellings together with its outstanding debt from one organisation to another

profit market: a market in in which profitability is maximised and policy provides a safety net for needs that cannot be satisfied by the profit motive

profit renting: a form of rental provision in which landlords attempt to charge the highest rents they can without competition from cost renting

ratchet effect: the vicious circle whereby increasing demand for owner occupation increases the pressure for more subsidies to enter owner occupation, which increases the demand for owner occupation

rent differential crisis: the problems caused to a dualist system when profit rents become significantly higher than cost rents

rent harmonisation problematic: the strain between demand-sensitive rents and the non-profit principle when integrating profit rents with immature cost renting in the transition to a unitary market

social market: a market in which a policy balance is struck and maintained between profitability and social needs

strategic policy area: a policy area in which changes in policy strategy have an important knock-on effect on other policy areas

unitary cost rental system: a unitary rental system in which cost renting eliminates profit rents

unitary part-profit rental system: a unitary rental system in which cost renting dampens profit rents

unitary rental system: a rental system in which cost and profit renting are allowed to compete with one another for households on comparable terms

Notes

PART I: INTRODUCTION

1 I use this as a shorthand adjective for English-speaking countries, devoid of its ethnic connotations (e.g. as distinct from celtic).

1 PROFIT MARKETS AND SOCIAL MARKETS

1 For a discussion of the patriarchal basis of classical economics see Pujol (1992).
2 'So called' because profit markets need to be constructed and maintained, and so non-intervention is in reality a self-justifying illusion.

2 THE ROMEO ERROR IN COMPARATIVE RENTING

1 Power also differs from both Harloe and Emms in not accepting the 'inevitability of decline' thesis of public renting. She argues emphatically for a continuing and even expanding future for social renting in industrial society.
2 Not necessarily both! There is an increasing tendency in some countries for social rental housing to generate surpluses that may be clawed back by government.

3 POLICY CONSTRUCTIVISM AND THE CONCEPT OF MATURATION

1 This definition of maturation is not to be confused with the concept of the maturation of a loan.

4 RECONCEPTUALISING RENTAL SYSTEMS

1 And a co-operative tenure combining owning and renting and comprising 17 per cent of the stock.
2 Like Germany and Denmark their public rental sectors are very residual

and they possess private rental sectors of around 20 per cent. This similarity is misleading, however. The crucial difference is that in Australia and New Zealand private renting is not exposed to competition from cost renting.

5   POWER, IDEOLOGY AND RENTAL MARKET POLICY STRUCTURING

1 It would be interesting to know whether the rental system in francophone Canada differs from the rest of Canada.
2 I am grateful to Stuart Lowe for drawing my attention to this issue.

6   CASE STUDIES IN THE MATURATION PROCESS

1 For a rare example of a study of cost rental housing using data of this sort see Bengtsson (1991). See also Kemeny (1980 and 1981c).
2 The Million Programme refers to a major housing construction effort supported by central government whereby one million new dwellings were to be built in the ten-year period 1965 to 1974.
3 It is also worth noting here that the takeover reduced the average debt load of Gavlegårdarna's stock to SEK 44,073 from the previous year's level of SEK 48,902 (see Table 4), a reduction of 11 per cent. This was due to the lower levels of indebtedness of Valbohem's disproportionately rural stock, with an average debt in its last year of operations (1970) of SEK 35,095.
4 It is possible that the data could be retrieved in some useable form even when it is in the form of unsorted bundles of memos and other council papers stacked in basements, as is often the case. But it would be a long and labour-intensive project.

7   COMMAND POLICIES

1 This discussion draws on Davidson (1992).
2 This discussion draws on Kemeny (1981a, pp. 112–29) and Kemeny (1983, pp. 50–6). See also Kemeny (1981b and 1981c).
3 The governor-general dismissed a majority Labor government when the upper house (where the opposition parties had a majority) blocked the Finance Bill and appointed a liberal government to hold a general election, which it won.
4 This is averaged over all tenants, including those in receipt of rent rebates. However, the total burden in fact falls on those tenants who receive no rent rebates and is therefore considerably heavier than this.

8   MARKET POLICIES

1 At the time of writing there is a surplus of vacant rental dwellings due to the economic recession, and so rents may not rise in the short run.

2 The data in this section are based on pre-unification West German statistics. I am grateful for information and unpublished data on the German rental market provided by Hartmut Haeussermann both personally and in Haeussermann (1991) upon which this section draws.
3 Although now reduced to 10 years for new housing, much earlier-built 25-year subsidy housing still remains.

10 FROM COMMAND ECONOMY TO THE SOCIAL MARKET

1 For very much earlier discussions see Kemeny (1981a, Chapter 9 on Britain and Australia) and Kemeny (1983, Chapter 7 on Australia).
2 Popular housing discourse is very revealing of the ideology that both reflects and reinforces the housing system. In dualist systems for most households 'permanent rental housing' is a contradiction in terms. In Australia it has long been common discourse to 'rent accommodation' but to 'buy a home'. A home is something one can only purchase, while accommodation is something one rents. This discourse is becoming increasingly established in Britain.

References

Andersen, Hans Skifter, Munk, Asger and Hansen, Knud Erik (1992) *Housing Policy, Urban Renewal and Social Housing in Germany*, Bulletin 94, National Building Research Institute, Hirsholm, Denmark.

Ball, Michael (1983) *Housing Policy and Economic Power: the political economy of owner occupation*, Macmillan, London.

Ball, Michael, Harloe, Michael and Martens, Maartje (1988) *Housing and Social Change in Europe and the USA*, Routledge, London.

Ball, Michael and Harloe, Michael (1992) 'Rhetorical barriers to understanding housing provision: what the "Provision Thesis" is and is not' *Housing Studies* 7(1): 3–15.

Balogh, Thomas (1950) *Germany: an experiment in 'planning' by the 'free' price mechanism*, Blackwell, Oxford.

Barry, Norman (1993) 'The social market economy', *Social Philosophy and Policy* 10(2): 1–25.

Bengtsson, Bo (1991) 'The crisis of public housing in Sweden – economic reality or organizational myth?', *Scandinavian Housing and Planning Research* 8(2) (special issue on comparative housing policy research): 113–27.

Bergenståhle, Sven (1982) *The Determination of Use Values and Rent Setting in Stockholm, Gothenburg and Malmö* (in Swedish), Swedish Council for Building Research R162, Stockholm.

Bowles, Samuel and Gintis, Herbert (1990) 'Contested exchange: new microfoundations for the political economy of capitalism', *Politics and Society* 18(2): 165–222.

Brouwer, Jan (1988) 'Rent policy in the Netherlands (1977–1985)', *The Netherlands Journal of Housing and Environmental Research* 3(4): 295–307.

Castells, Manuel (1977) *The Urban Question: a marxist approach*, Matthew Arnold, London [1976].

Castles, Francis (1978) *The Social Democratic Image of Society*, Routledge, London.

Cooper, Stephanie (1985) *Public Housing and Private Profit*, Ashgate, Brookfield VT.

Cox, R.H. (1993) 'Creating welfare states in Czechoslovakia and Hungary: why policymakers borrow ideas from the West', *Environment and Planning C* 11(3): 349–64.

Davidson, Alexander (1992) 'A home of one's own: housing policy in Sweden and New Zealand 1840–1990', Department of Government, Uppsala University (unpublished).

Elander, Ingemar (1991) 'Good dwellings for all: the case of social rented housing in Sweden', *Housing Studies* 6(1): 29–43.

Emms, Peter (1990) *Social Housing: a European dilemma?*, Occasional Paper, School for Advanced Urban Studies, Bristol.

Esping-Andersen, Gøsta (1985) *Politics against Markets: the social democratic road to power*, Princeton University Press, Princeton NJ.

Esping-Andersen, Gøsta (1990) *The Three Worlds of Welfare Capitalism*, Polity Press, Cambridge.

Fligstein, Neil (1990) *The Transformation of Corporate Control*, Harvard University Press, Cambridge MA.

Granovetter, Mark (1973) 'The strength of weak ties', *American Journal of Sociology* 78: 1360–80.

Granovetter, Mark (1983) 'The strength of weak ties revisited', in Randall Collins (ed.) *Sociological Theory*, Jossey-Bass, San Francisco CA, 201–33.

Granovetter, Mark (1985) 'Economic action and social structure: the problem of embeddedness', *American Journal of Sociology* 91(3): 481–510.

Gray, John (1993) 'From post-communism to civil society: the re-emergence of history and the decline of the western model', *Social Philosophy and Policy* 10(2): 26–50.

Gurtner, P. (1988) 'Switzerland', in Hans Kroes, Fritz Ymkers and André Mulder (eds) *Between Owner Occupation and the Rented Sector: Housing in ten European countries*, The Netherlands Christian Institute for Social Housing, De Bilt, The Netherlands, 351–95.

Haeussermann, Hartmut (1991) 'Housing and social policy in Germany', paper presented at the Research Conference on Rented Housing in Europe, Örebro, August 1992 (cyclostyled).

Harloe, Michael (1978) 'The Green Paper on Housing Policy', in M. Brown (ed.) *Yearbook of Social Policy 1978*, Routledge & Kegan Paul, London.

Harloe, Michael (1985) *Private Rented Housing in the United States and Europe*, Routledge, London.

Harloe, Michael (1993) 'Social housing: residualisation or reformation?', paper prepared for the European Network for Housing Research Conference 'Housing Policy in Europe in the 1990s', Budapest, September 1993.

Jones, M.A. (1972) *Housing and Society in Australia*, Melbourne University Press, Melbourne.

Kemeny, Jim (1980) 'The South Australian Housing Trust: a socio-economic case study of public housing', *Australian Journal of Social Issues* 15(2): 108–34.

Kemeny, Jim (1981a) *The Myth of Home Ownership: public versus private choices in housing tenure*, Routledge, London.

Kemeny, Jim (1981b) 'Controlling public renting: structure and process in Australian public housing', *Australian and New Zealand Journal of Sociology* 17(2): 4–9.

Kemeny, Jim (1981c) 'The cost of selling public rental housing: Victoria and South Australia compared', *Australian Journal of Social Issues* 16(4): 297–312.

188   *References*

Kemeny, Jim (1983a) *The Great Australian Nightmare: a critique of the home ownership ideology*, Georgian House, Melbourne.

Kemeny, Jim (1983b) *The Privatised City: critical studies in Australian housing and urban structure*, CURS Occasional Paper 10, Birmingham University.

Kemeny, Jim (1992a) *Housing and Social Theory*, Routledge, London.

Kemeny, Jim (1992b) 'Swedish social renting in comparative perspective: a critique of recent work', School for Advanced Urban Studies Working Paper 107, University of Bristol.

Kemeny, Jim (1992c) 'Swedish rent-setting policy: labour-led corporatism in a strategic policy area', *International Journal of Urban and Regional Research* 16(4): 555–70.

Kemeny, Jim (1993) 'The significance of Swedish rental policy: cost renting command economy versus the social market in comparative perspective', *Housing Studies* 8(1): 3–15.

Klunder, Ruud (1988) 'Private financing in the Dutch public housing sector: the rise and fall of the accumulative loan', *The Netherlands Journal of Housing and Environmental Research* 3(4): 309–18.

Korpi, Walter (1978) *The Working Class in Welfare Capitalism*, Routledge & Kegan Paul, London.

Korpi, Walter (1983) *The Democratic Class Struggle*, Routledge & Kegan Paul, London.

Lehmbruch, Gerhard (1984) 'Concertation and the structure of corporatist networks', in John H. Goldthorpe (ed.) *Order and Conflict in Contemporary Capitalism*, Clarendon Press, Oxford, 60–80.

Leutner, Bernd and Jensen, Dagmar (1988) 'German Federal Republic', in Hans Kroes, Fritz Ymkers and André Mulder (eds) *Between Owner Occupation and the Rented Sector: Housing in ten European countries*, The Netherlands Christian Institute for Social Housing, De Bilt, The Netherlands, 145–81.

Lijphart, Arend and Crepaz, Markus M.L. (1991) 'Corporatism and consensus democracy in eighteen countries: conceptual and empirical linkages', *British Journal of Political Science* 21(2): 235–246.

Lundqvist, L.J., Elander, I. and Danemark, B. (1990) 'Housing policy in Sweden – still a success story?', *International Journal of Urban and Regional Research* 14: 445–67.

Malpass, Peter (1990) *Reshaping Housing Policy: subsidies, rents and residualisation*, Routledge, London.

Malpass, Peter, Warburton, Matthew, Bramley, Glen and Smart, Gavin (1993) *Housing Policy in Action: the new financial regime for council housing*, School for Advanced Urban Studies Occasional Paper, Bristol.

Margolis, Howard (1993) *Paradigms and Barriers: how habits of mind govern scientific beliefs*, University of Chicago Press, Chicago.

Matznetter, Walter (1992) 'Organizational networks in a corporatist housing system: non-profit housing associations and housing politics in Vienna, Austria', in *Scandinavian Housing and Planning Research*, Supplement 2 (special issue on the comparative history of housing in small welfare states), 23–35.

Meyer, Fritz W. (1989) 'Development aid in a free market system', in Alan Peacock and Hans Willgerodt (eds) *Germany's Social Market Economy: origins and evolution*, Macmillan, London, 242–60.

Meyerson, Per-Martin, Ståhl, Ingemar and Wickman, Kurt (1990) *Power over Housing* (in Swedish), SNS Förlag, Stockholm.

Müller-Armack, Alfred (1989) 'The meaning of the social market economy', in Alan Peacock and Hans Willgerodt (eds) *Germany's Social Market Economy: origins and evolution*, Macmillan, London, 82–6.

Murie, Alan (1993) 'Privatization and restructuring public involvement in housing provision in Britain', *Scandinavian Housing and Planning Research* 10(3): 145–57.

New Zealand (1953) *Parliamentary Debates* (11 Sept.) p. 100, Government of New Zealand, Wellington.

Power, Anne (1993) *Hovels to High Rise: state housing in Europe since 1850*, Routledge, London.

Pujol, Michele A. (1992) *Feminism and Anti-Feminism in Early Economic Thought*, Edward Elgar, Aldershot.

Raynsford, Nick (1992) 'Arm's length companies: an option for local authority housing', *Housing Review* 41(2): 26–8.

Rex, John and Moore, R. (1967) *Race, Community and Conflict*, Oxford University Press, Oxford.

Röpke, Wilhelm (1950) *The Social Crisis of Our Time*, University of Chicago Press, Chicago (trans. A. and P. Schiffer Jacobsohn) [1942].

Rothstein, B. (1987) 'Corporatism and reformism: the social democratic institutionalization of class conflict', *Acta Sociologica* 30(3–4): 295–312.

Ruonavaara, Hannu (1987) 'The Kemeny approach and the case of Finland', *Scandinavian Housing and Planning Research* 4(3): 163–77.

Saunders, Peter (1990) *A Nation of Home Owners*, Unwin Hyman, London.

Schmitter, Phillippe C. (1982) 'Reflections on where the theory of corporatism has gone and where the praxis of neo-corporatism may be going', in G. Lehmbruch and P.C. Schmitter (eds) *Patterns of Corporate Policymaking*, Sage, London.

Silver, Allan (1990) 'Friendship in commercial society: eighteenth century social theory and modern sociology', *American Journal of Sociology*, 95(6): 1475–1504.

Skocpol, Theda (1993) 'Gender and the origins of modern social policy', *Vilhelm Aubert Memorial Lecture 1992*, Institute for Social Research, University of Oslo.

Stephens, John (1979) *The Transition from Capitalism to Socialism*, Macmillan, London.

Sveinsson, Jon Runar (1993) 'Housing in the reluctant Icelandic welfare state', paper presented at the 17th Nordic Congress of Sociology, Gävle, Sweden.

Tilton, Tim (1990) *The Political Theory of Swedish Social Democracy: through the welfare state to socialism*, Clarendon Press, Oxford.

Torgersen, Ulf (1987) 'Housing: the wobbly pillar under the welfare state', in Bengt Turner, Jim Kemeny and Lennart Lundqvist (eds) *Between State and Market: housing in the post-industrial era*, Almqvist and Wicksell International.

Turner, Bengt (1979) *Rent-setting in the Housing Market: from rent control to use values* (in Swedish), Swedish Building Research Council, Report 69, Stockholm.

Turner, Bengt (1983) *Rents and Rent Policy in Sweden* (in Swedish), National Swedish Institute for Building Research Bulletin, M83: 8, Gävle.

Warner, Kee and Molotch, Harvey (1993) 'Information on the marketplace: media explanations of the '87 crash', *Social Problems* 40(2): 167–88.

Wilensky, Harold L. (1975) *The Welfare State and Equality: structural and ideological roots of public expenditure*, University of California Press, Berkeley CA.

Willgerodt, Hans and Peacock, Alan (1989) 'German liberalism and economic revival', in Alan Peacock and Hans Willgerodt (eds) *Germany's Social Market Economy: origins and evolution*, Macmillan, London, 1–14.

Wilson, Frank L. (1983) 'Interest groups and politics in Western Europe: the neo-corporatist approach', *Comparative Politics* 16(1): 105–23.

Wright Mills, C. (1970) *The Sociological Imagination*, Pelican, London [1959].

Index